Bank

for

Steelhead & Salmon

by Scott Haugen

Bank Fishing for Steelhead & Salmon

by Scott Haugen

Frank Amato
PORTLAND

Dedication

To all those anglers beginning to explore the great joys salmon and steelhead fishing has to offer, this book is for you. And for those seasoned anglers hoping to gain a bit more of an edge, the words in these pages were also chosen with you in mind.

Were it not for you, the angler, there would be no need for this book. Having pursued salmon and steelhead since the mid-1960s, I feel honored to be able to share some of the important keys I've learned over my years on the water.

Good Fishing and God Bless,

Scott Haugen

Acknowledgments

In my eyes, I have the best job in the world. Being able to make a living from the outdoors is a dream come true, and I'm very thankful. At the same time, it's not easy. I'm not the kind of person who approaches any task with mediocrity. If I can't do a job with 100% effort and dedication, then it's not worth doing.

As a full-time outdoorsman it's important to me that I be in the field as much as possible. That's how I learn, and what I learn I like to share with fellow anglers—that's just the way I am, maybe it has something to do with my being a school teacher for 12 years before getting into this business.

Due to the demands I put on myself, I'm in the field a lot; more than 250 days most years. With this much time spent afield, sacrifices are made. I watch virtually no TV during the year, I don't do parties and I don't hang out at college football games on Saturdays.

Any spare time I have—and it's not enough—is spent with my family. Without their continued support and unconditional love, I would not be able to do this job, and for that I am forever grateful to them.

I would like to thank my parents, Jerry and Jean Haugen, for all they've taught me over the years. They were the ones who instilled a strong work ethic and solid moral standards within me at an early age. To my two sons, Braxton and Kazden, their enthusiasm always keeps me going. And to my wife, Tiffany, her ongoing love and always-positive spirit make it possible for me to keep going. Without all of this support from the home, I would not be able to do this blessed job. Thank you!

All inquiries should be addressed to:
Frank Amato Publications, Inc.
P.O. Box 82112
Portland, OR 97282
(503) 653-8108 • www.amatobooks.com

All photos taken by the author unless otherwise noted
Cover design by Tony Amato • Book design by Nick Amato

SB ISBN-10: 1-57188-456-4   SB ISBN-13: 978-1-57188-456-5   SB UPC: 0-81127-00295-5
Printed in Singapore

10 9 8 7 6 5 4 3 2

Contents

Introduction

I once heard of a survey that said nearly 20% of new anglers enter into the sport of salmon and steelhead fishing every year. That's a big number: one-fifth of the total fishing crowd, to be exact.

I remember the very first steelhead I caught, back in 1968. I was exploring the beautiful banks of Oregon's North Umpqua River, when I lost track of where I was, slipped and fell into the river. Fortunately it was mid-summer, and, yes, I did have a lifejacket on.

After a few swats to my backside, and a little time to think about it, Dad encouraged me to grab my rod and get to fishing. The very next cast I caught my first summer steelhead. A chrome-bright fish took me all over the river. It was more exciting than I ever imagined. A few casts later I caught another, and was done for the day.

From that moment on I was hooked. I was only four years old.

Years later, both of my sons would also catch their first summer steelhead, both at the age of four. It was more exciting living the experience of Braxton's and Kazden's first catches than mine. Shortly after that, they'd both catch their first chinook salmon.

Any time a new angler enters into the world of salmon and steelhead fishing, they look for guidance. There are many questions to be answered, and only so many places to turn. Fellow anglers are, perhaps, the best teaching tool for new anglers.

BANK FISHING FOR STEELHEAD & SALMON

Unfortunately, many seasoned anglers scoff at having more anglers, especially "new" ones on the water. But the fact is, our long-term survival as sportsmen is based on how many active members we have within our fraternity. The more anglers we can recruit—no matter what their age—the better.

Of the 20% of newcomers to the sport, virtually all begin by fishing from the bank. From there, the natural progression is to invest in a drift boat, then a sled or motorized boat. Still, however, when accounting for all the salmon and steelhead anglers out there, the large majority actually fish from the bank.

The purpose of this book is to educate bank anglers who are looking to get into salmon and steelhead fishing. It doesn't matter whether it's summer or winter steelhead, spring or fall chinook, king salmon in Alaska, cohos, chums, pinks or red salmon, this book will help you catch more fish.

We'll take a close look at steps that can be taken to maximize your overall efficiency, use of time on and off the water, and what gear is involved. We'll also detail specific fishing techniques, and, perhaps most importantly, learn how to read the water being fished.

Finally, we'll consider available options to increase bank fishing success. If you're a newcomer to salmon and steelhead fishing, the information within these pages is sure to be of help. Of course, the less you know, the more you have to learn, and that's where the information in these pages will truly shine.

Chapter 1

Home Preparation

Before even hitting the water there's work to be done at home. In fact, some anglers consider time spent at home to be among the most valuable, for this sets the tone for how your day on the water will go. Based on personal experience, it's safe to say, the more organized and prepared you are, the more fishing time you'll get, and the greater your chances will be of catching more fish.

While setting up rods and organizing terminal gear are a couple key steps to be done at home, there is also a degree of homework that needs to be carried out. This homework includes researching the best rivers to fish at the time, learning where bank fishing access exists on those rivers, then determining which techniques will best help you catch fish.

Let's start with the rivers.

River Research

When learning where to fish a river for the first time, there are many considerations to take into account. One of the best ways to learn a river or section of river is by studying a map of the system. Maps provide an orientation as to how a river lays in accordance with the surrounding landscapes. Such basic information can greatly influence where you choose to fish, and how.

Some maps even lay out the best bank fishing locations and how to access them. Some locations may be right off a main road, while others may require a bit of a hike. The key here is finding information that appeals to how you want to fish.

For example, anglers who have no friends that fish and are learning all on their own may opt to fish among the crowds. The reason for this is getting to know and learn from the locals. Overall, anglers are a happy group of people, and if you're honest and up front about wanting to learn from them, I know very few who will turn you down. For this reason alone, many new anglers choose to fish among the crowds.

Learning all you can about a river, before fishing it, will greatly aid in your overall efficiency.

On the other hand, if you're looking for a secluded fishing spot where you can learn through trial and error, many maps can point you in the right direction. There are several ways to go about getting maps, and they come in many forms and degrees of detail.

No matter what the target species, the more you know about the river being fished, the condition it's in and how you'll fish it, the higher your catch rates will be. Haugen targeted this big chum in a clear travel route.

Good maps showing river descriptions, including ramps, areas of caution, even prime fishing holes, are available at sporting goods stores. Books such as the *Atlas & Gazetteer* series are good resources. Many local stores carry maps made by independent companies or individuals, capturing outstanding details and offering local knowledge that's tough to get anywhere else.

But those books penned by fishing authors or publishers are likely the most beneficial. Frank Amato Publications publishes some excellent map books packed with comprehensive details. Other book publishers offer map-related titles, and fishing magazines with map feature stories are always good resources to hang on to. Many magazine publishers stockpile past issues; ordering issues with river map features can help you establish a solid library, quickly.

With our growing technology, websites also have valuable information based on maps of specific rivers. Some state agencies may keep up-to-date map information on rivers in their area, which can also help.

Maps are a great investment, and learning can continue from them for several years. Once you start catching fish from such rivers, keep track of where they come from, on the map or in a journal. As seasons pass, make it a point to reference the places you've previously caught fish. It's also a good idea to make a note of what gear you catch fish on and what the water and weather conditions were like at the time of the catch. Maps and information you record which centers around them, really are a valuable resource that takes years off the learning curve.

King Salmon Fishing Prohibited

Except 5 weekends and Mondays starting weekend before Memorial Day

Fishing Allowed Except for King Salmon July 1 to Dec 31

Closed to all Fishing
January 1 to weekend before Memorial Day

•*Rainbow/Steelhead catch & release only*
•*Artificial lures only Sept 1 to Dec 31*
•*Check regulations for boundary markers & details*

Written, updated laws posted along rivers are the responsibility of anglers to be aware of.

Accurately tracking river levels can be very important in helping catch fish in the future. The information can get pretty detailed; keeping a log or journal is wise. It's helpful to note, for instance, what the river level and conditions are when fish start arriving in a river. It's also good to know what are considered prime water levels for bank fishing in each river you fish, even within certain sections of a river. Each river has a very fishable level for ideal bank fishing and noting what these levels are is important. Once the levels get too low or too high, the fishing action slows.

On one river I fish, the ideal bank fishing level is 4.5 to 5.5 feet, about a mile above tidewater. On another river, when the level is 5.6 to 6.0 feet at tidewater, the fishing is good about 20 miles upstream. By keeping track of which levels make for ideal fishing on all the rivers you fish, you'll become dialed-in to when you're likely to catch the most fish. Timing is very important.

Once you've studied a river and know you want to fish it, it's time to delve into the fishing regulations for that system. This may seem like a technicality, but it's the law, and each year numerous beginning anglers are slapped with fines for unknowingly breaking the law. Following the rules is your responsibility.

Every year, each state releases a booklet of fishing regulations. As soon as these regulations come out, pick up a copy and read through the parts that apply to the waters you want to fish. If it's a stream you've fished in the past, look for changes that may have taken place. There are regulations relating to both rivers and gear, so read carefully.

Regulations are the written laws by which anglers must abide when on the water. It's our responsibility to know the information in them, as well as apply what they say.

In addition to the primary regulations, keep an eye and ear out for any unprinted changes which may go into effect. As season's progress in many rivers, catch rates, run numbers and escapements over dams are just some factors that can warrant a sudden change in regulations. Prior to wetting a line, check bulletin boards, signs or even fliers posted on trees or telephone poles, updating anglers with the most relevant information and regulatory changes. Look in diners, gas stations, local sporting goods stores, fish and wildlife websites for regulation updates. Radio and television spots are also good sources through which to monitor such changes.

It's our responsibility to know the laws and any changes in the laws which may appear during the course of a season. As law-abiding anglers it's our obligation to promote ethical practices and uphold the laws—the least we can do is take time to know these laws and how they apply to waters we're fishing.

Once you know the lay of the river and the laws which apply to it, it's time to track what the water is doing a day or two prior to actually fishing it. One of the biggest mistakes I see being made, especially during those winter steelheading months when river levels quickly fluctuate, is anglers fishing a river without knowing exactly what the conditions are like.

No matter what the time of year, checking river levels before heading afield is wise. Several things can influence how much water is flowing in a river, thus impacting clarity levels and overall fishing. Rain storms, quick snow melt, emergency openings of dams, the operation of irrigation canals, even tributary activity impacts the level of a river. Not only can this effect if you'll fish, but how you'll fish.

During the rainy months it's especially important to inquire about river levels. This is the time of year when conditions can change overnight, and tracking storm systems can save many hours of frustration. There are many regional websites that lead to river-level monitoring stations, and they are updated frequently which makes them a valuable information source. Radio, television and newspapers can also offer information worth knowing, depending on the rivers being sought. Some regions still offer telephone hotlines which can direct you to specific streams, though the shift is leading toward computer referencing. Typing in a simple search of river levels for the area you plan to fish can yield quick, informative results. State fish and wildlife agencies can also help point you in the right direction, as can fish hatchery personnel.

Knowing how much water is flowing through a system can dictate how you fish, so, by being aware of what's happening you'll be better prepared to use the most applicable approaches which will allow you to find fish. For example,

Knowing precise water levels will help you determine where the fish are, thus how you should go about fishing for them.

you may not be a plunking fan, but if the river is high and off-color, it's going to make for tough jig-fishing. At the same time, if the river is low, those giant drift-bobbers may not be necessary. If a river is running exceptionally low and clear, it may be best to switch to fluorocarbon leader, so as not to risk spooking fish. Be aware of what the river is doing and adjust accordingly.

Though there's not a great deal of tidally influenced bank

Sharon Manente moved upstream of the tidal push, escaped crowds and found plenty of fish.

taken place. A big tide may find you closer to the river's mouth if you want to get into those fish quickly, and if there is bank access that low in the system.

On the other hand, if you don't want to battle crowds, you may want to wait for the fish to come to you a bit further upstream. If fishing tidal zones, be sure to reference the most up-to-date tide books; these are available for a nominal fee at local and regional sporting goods stores, as well as area marinas. If fishing near a marina, the folks there are usually very helpful in terms of offering information as to when the fishing is best, based on the given tidal conditions. When reading tide books, make certain to adjust for times as instructed, if necessary. By noting tidal fluctuation times, your fishing time can be spent in the best locations.

With all the aforementioned aspects to keep track of, the best resources from which to learn may be people, namely fellow anglers. Sporting goods store personnel as well as tackle shop owners and hatchery staff members are often dialed-in to the hottest action. In

fishing, there is some, which means that tides should also be checked. Over the years, from small coastal streams in the Pacific Northwest, through British Columbia and around Alaska, I've caught a good number of steelhead, coho and chinook from the bank in strong, tidally influenced rivers. On one of my most memorable trips to Alaska, I hit the head of an incoming tide and got into some of the best spring steelheading action I've ever experienced. It wouldn't have happened were I not closely watching the tides.

The exact time a tidal shift occurs and the magnitude of that shift are two important variables to consider when targeting tidewater fish. Another key point to weigh is how far upstream you intend on fishing once a tide change has

Tracking river conditions is one of the most important responsibilities salmon and steelhead anglers have.

rural areas, diners, gas stations and marinas can be a valuable aid. If you don't know someone who lives in or has been fishing the area you'd like to visit, give one of these resources a call.

Ask about river conditions, the number of fish showing up, what they're hitting on and where. One phone call can save hours of driving and an entire day of fishing in the wrong spot. These lines of communication can help direct you to where the best action is, and hopefully a productive day on the water. Local fish and wildlife agencies are also valued help.

Don't overlook fishing-related websites that often file timely reports, including the posting of river conditions. Site-specific chat rooms and blogs can also help direct you to the right destination; it's a great feeling knowing there are others out there wanting to help you succeed on the water.

Organize Gear

Some of the best anglers I've had the pleasure of fishing with are also the most organized. These folks set themselves apart from the rest of the crowd by being prepared to make quick gear transitions in a moment's notice. They're also prepared to offer fish a wide array of presentations and try several different forms of gear. The result is maximized fishing time on the water, which leads to more fish being caught.

Well before setting foot on the river bank, take the necessary time at home to make sure everything is in order. You can start anywhere, just make sure you have all your bases covered. It's a good idea to have a checklist in place, so all you have to do is quickly go over it at the last minute to make sure you have everything you'll need. I know guides who do this with a big dry-erase

By being organized with his research and gear, Haugen was able to experience exceptional action on these fresh pink salmon.

board. They write in permanent marker what they'll need, then check off with an erasable marker what they've got in order before every trip. It's very efficient and works well. You can also do the same with paper and pen.

I don't know how many times over the years I've set out, sure I had all the gear I needed, only to discover that wasn't the case. Usually this comes at the most inopportune time, like when I'm standing chest-deep in a riffle, and find I don't have any of my pre-tied leaders. The point is, any angler, no matter what their level of

Carrying pre-tied leaders in an easily accessible container will increase fishing time when on the water.

experience, can overlook even the most common tackle. This can lead to lost fishing time, even money if you've traveled any distance to reach your destination.

Let's start with pre-tying leaders. One of the biggest wastes of time on the water is tying on fresh terminal gear every time it breaks off. Rather than starting this process from scratch, and wasting a few minutes each time, have leaders pre-tied and ready to go. Then you'll only have to tie one knot.

I like having an array of pre-tied leaders to fit the many conditions in which I may find myself. For instance, if fishing winter steelhead, water conditions can vary greatly from one river to another, even from

one day to the next. For reasons such as these, I like being prepared, accordingly. If fishing in high, turbid waters for winter steelhead, I like a 12-pound leader with a 2/0 hook. If fishing low, clear water, I may drop down to 10-pound, fluorocarbon leader with a size-2 hook.

Generally, it's a good idea to have three or four different leader set-ups for each fish species, for each season. It's also a good idea to tie a variety of yarn colors onto these leaders, so they are ready to retie the moment you lose a rigging. It's basic. Using leader keepers, simply store the leaders by line class weight and clearly label them. It takes time to get pre-tied leaders in order, but it's time saved on the water.

As soon as you get home from a fishing trip, it's a good idea to replace all the gear you lost. This will ensure you'll have it for the next time out. One step many anglers take is purchasing multiple items of their favorite gear, so they can replace it from home. If, for instance, you found your favorite-colored spinner at the store, rather than buying just one, get a few, so you can replace them when lost. Oftentimes we don't get home from a trip until late at night, when stores are closed, and if you're heading out the following morning, having extra gear already in-hand will ensure you have what you need to help catch more fish.

Keeping your tackle box organized is also a good idea. There are many ways to go about this, but when it comes to bank fishing, the rule I follow is: Keep it light! The more gear you have to tote around, the less mobile you become. Of course, there are exceptions to this rule, but they are few.

At home, try keeping all of your gear organized in one tackle box. If you spend a lot of time on the river, then you may want to invest in multiple tackle boxes. For instance, many anglers have a separate tackle box each for spring chinook, fall chinook, summer steelhead and winter steelhead. Their reasoning is right on, all they have to do is grab the tackle box they want for the given species they'll be going after, and they're ready to go.

One thing you will learn as time goes on is that each species of fish requires different gear, so it makes sense to have the specialized items for the fish you'll be targeting. If you don't have the space or money to invest in multiple tackle box set-ups, there is another option.

Rather than having multiple tackle boxes, try using peg boards on one of your garage or shop walls. Organize your tackle on the peg boards so you know where everything is and it's easy to get to. This is how I organize my tackle, and it works great. All I have to do is replace my lost gear as needed,

When organizing your gear, realize that each species of fish may have different requirements. By keeping all your gear straight, you'll be better prepared to hit the river and make sure you're not overlooking anything.

and my tackle is visible at all times, so I know exactly what I have, and don't have.

From the peg boards, all you have to do is grab your tackle and go. For bank fishing, this is simple as you're usually traveling very light, anyway.

There are several ways for bank anglers to carry their gear to the fishing site, but the key is remembering to stay mobile. The more fishing experience you gain,

When bank fishing, don't weigh yourself down with too much gear. Take only what you need to get the job done.

the more familiar you'll become with knowing what gear you need and what you don't need.

For example, I know that in one of my favorite summer-steelhead fishing rivers where there are lots of hang-ups, I can plan on losing upwards of two dozen riggings a day. In another of my favorite holes, I know I'll likely only lose a few riggings each day. If spending time at these locations, I'll gear-up accordingly.

One of the biggest mistakes I see bank anglers make is toting along too much gear. Not only does this cost them travel time when walking the bank, searching for a fishing spot, but it also cuts down on the amount of water they can cover. Not many people like carrying a hefty tackle box and net any great distance, then cart back a limit of salmon or steelhead, along with all that gear, on the way out.

When bank fishing, try and carry your gear on your person. Personally,

I like having two bait boxes that I strap to my belt and carry on each side of my waist. In one I'll put all the sinkers, swivels, beads, drift-bobbers, lures and any other terminal gear I may need on that day. In the other box, I'll put all my baits: cured eggs, sand shrimp, sardine strips, etc. My leaders are usually carried in my back pants pocket, allowing quick and easy access.

When summer steelhead fishing, where gear requirements are light, try downsizing to two small bait boxes. This makes for easier travel. If strapping bait boxes to your waist is not appealing, then try a fly-fishing vest. With its multiple pockets and large pouch in the back, a fly vest is perfect for the gear angler.

Backpacks or fanny packs are also a good choice. Some companies make backpacks specifically designed for bank anglers. When going to places like Alaska or Canada, this pack becomes my complete tackle box and holds enough gear for weeks of fishing. Hunting style backpacks with their multiple pockets also work well when it comes to holding and accessing large amounts of gear. Packs are great for salmon fishing, in particular, where more gear is generally required than for steelheading.

If not wanting to carry a full-sized backpack, try a fanny pack. Some fanny packs are specifically designed for bank anglers. Between a fanny pack, pant and jacket pockets, you can usually carry all the gear you'll need.

If wearing waders, often the zippered pouches in front offer enough room to carry all your gear. The only glitch you may run into is where to carry bait. If wading deep, try to keep the bait on your person—you don't want to waste time wading back to shore to re-bait your hook every time it's needed. Simply place the bait in a sturdy, sealable baggy and carry in a pouch, or strap a bait box on your wader belt, and you're set.

Whatever transport system you choose to carry your gear in, make sure it allows you to make quick and easy gear changes. Bank anglers lose a great deal of fishing time when they tie themselves to the bank, so don't let this happen. If wading in the river, the last thing you want to do to re-rig or bait-up

is walk back to shore and waste time digging through your gear. By keeping the tackle on your person, you can make any and all gear changes while in the water. Not only will this save time, it will prevent other anglers from infringing on your water in those pressured holes and it will also lessen the risk of spooking fish.

Another home-based tip is making sure to clean your towels. Salmon and steelhead have incredible noses, and they can detect even the most subtle of foul odors. Their sniffers are so good,

Specialized fishing backpacks allow much gear to be stored in an organized fashion. Haugen relied on all the gear in this pack to last him three weeks while fishing in Alaska.

Simple backpacks can increase the mobility of a bank angler.

they can smell in parts per billion. This means it's important to keep things clean.

I always carry a towel or two with me when on the water. This allows me to keep my gear and hands clean. When handling gooey eggs and fish, towels are essential. I simply clip it onto my pants for easy transport. Once you get home, be sure to toss the rags in the washer and get them clean. This will ensure rotting blood, fish slime and other bacterial attractants are gone for the next trip out. It's a good idea to have several clean towels stored and ready to go when you are.

Bait Preparation

The preparation of baits is another task that can be carried out at home. Obviously, baits will normally be cured at home, as the processes can be long and tedious. Whether curing eggs, shrimp, baitfish, crayfish, squid or more,

getting it done at home is the most sensible option.

But once these baits are cured, make sure they are ready to fish. Clearly label all cured baits with the date cured, type of cure used and kind of bait. For example, the egg clusters you use on summer steelhead will be much smaller than those used on salmon. Some cures will carry different ingredients for different target fish, as well. The list goes on, but the key remains the same: know what bait you're fishing.

If thawing baits that have been frozen, make sure to do so ahead of time. The last thing you want is to get caught on the water with frozen bait, as you'll lose valuable fishing time. If thawing bait for winter steelhead, and it's cold outside, know that it may take a day or two for them to thaw. If thawing baits for summer fishing, know they'll thaw quickly.

When thawing baits, do it slowly. Avoid placing frozen baits

18

Having good eggs that milk out well is a top priority when fishing with bait, especially for salmon.

in direct sunlight or near heaters, as quickly thawing them results in broken-down tissue which means the baits fall apart when being fished. Many anglers equate this to a poor curing recipe, when, in fact, it was the thawing process that caused the eggs to degenerate. For the best results, thaw baits in a cool, dark corner of the garage or in a refrigerator. The more slowly frozen baits can be thawed, the more productive they'll be when fished.

If buying baits, do it ahead of time. It's frustrating to pull in to the mini-market in the wee hours of the morning, only to discover they're clean out of bait...I know,

I've been there. Plan ahead and prepare accordingly. There's nothing wrong with buying baits a couple days ahead of the planned fishing trip, as long as it's fresh and kept refrigerated, you should be okay.

When it comes to maximizing your fishing time, the most important steps start at home. Think and plan ahead, and gear-up according to your specific needs. Based on the information you acquired when researching what water to fish, you'll be able to make wise decisions on which gear and methods will work best. Knowing these valuable pieces of information is important to long-term success, and can be figured out at home.

Chapter 2:

Reading Water

Successfully fishing for salmon and steelhead is like an ongoing puzzle. That's because to continually and successfully catch salmon and steelhead requires the coming together of many elements. From learning where to fish, to knowing how to fish and much more, every piece of information is crucial to the overall big picture of success.

Each piece of the fish-catching

Reading the water is of utmost importance when it comes to catching nice fish like this. Don Newman photo

puzzle is important, though some pieces are more important than others. Reading water is one of those vital pieces. No matter how fancy your gear, how much you know about a river and the fish that reside in it, it's all of little value if you can't read the water.

Reading water is one of those facets of the sport that's difficult to capture in words. The best way

to learn how to read water is by spending time on the river, learning by trial and error. Observing fellow anglers, paying close attention to where and how they fish, will also be of great help in learning to interpret the water and decipher where fish will be.

That said, let's take a look at how to at least get started reading water. In the chapters that follow, we'll delve into the gear and specific techniques used while fishing for salmon and steelhead. But let's jump right in to the most important element: reading the water.

When reading water, the angler is looking at the surface features in an attempt to decipher what's happening under the surface. From there, the angler then has to figure out where the fish are, and deduce why. Then, they have to figure out how to catch the fish based on the information they've interpreted.

Because salmon and steelhead occupy different habitats within their aquatic environments, let's take a look at

Salmon and steelhead often occupy different waters, and knowing where to find both is key to consistent success.

each species based on the specific water types they inhabit.

We'll start with salmon, then look at steelhead.

Salmon: Holding Water

When salmon enter a river system, they either hold in one spot or travel to another spot. The moment salmon commit to swimming up a freshwater stream, it's the beginning of the end for them. Their bodies shut down to the point where they no longer actively feed, which is a big switch from their predatory lifestyle at sea. This also makes it challenging for anglers to get these fish to bite.

They begin absorbing their fatty tissue, decreasing their need to survive off fresh foods. Everything a salmon does from this point on revolves around their preparation to spawn, then they die. Unlike steelhead, every salmon perishes soon after spawning.

Chinook salmon holding water, if unchanged, can produce fish for years on end. Here, the author's wife, Tiffany, admires a salmon taken in a shallow holding spot.

There are many factors that can cause a salmon to shift position in a single hole throughout the course of the day. Being aware of these factors, and knowing how to adjust your fishing style is important.

Depending on the river system being fished, salmon can hold in different types of water. In rivers with deep sections, it's the deep, swirling holes wherein salmon stage. On shallow, faster-moving systems, salmon can seek rest in a mere foot or two deep, graveled depression. Knowing where salmon hold, and why, is crucial to catching them.

Deep, swirling holes are perhaps the best known, and most frequently occupied holding spots for salmon, especially chinook, coho and chum salmon. These deep swirl holes are where a large number of salmon are caught.

Two of the best salmon holes I grew up fishing are still producing. They are on two different rivers, and the salmon keg-up in them every year. Not matter if the water is high or low, clear or murky, the salmon always hold in them. Not only have I been catching salmon from these holes for years, but my father and grandfathers all caught fish from these spots before I was even born. My family has been catching salmon from these holes since the 1940s, to be exact. That shows how productive deep salmon holes can be if the rivers don't change.

There are two important factors to know when it comes to targeting salmon in deep holes. First, fish will change their position during the course of the day. Second, when they do change positions, this can change how to fish for them.

Generally speaking, early morning finds most salmon gathered at the head end, or the upstream side, of big swirl holes. This is because salmon do most of their migrating at night, but in rivers where they don't have far to travel, they may stay in one hole for days, even weeks, on end. Still, their instincts tell them to swim upstream in the dark, but often they only go as far as where the deep hole is met by fast flowing water. This means you'll want to fish the upper end of the deep hole at first light.

As the day progresses, both fishing pressure and sunlight can force salmon into the deeper places of the hole. If the hole is deep and swirling, the fish may actually suspend, meaning they won't necessarily hold tight to the bottom. This is where fishing bait suspended beneath a float can be highly effective.

If an eye of a swirl forms, this is a good starting point to focus your fishing efforts. The eye is created where the water swirls and actually reverses direction. Fish can actually hold with their noses facing downstream in these situations because they are nosing into the current, and if the swirl is big enough, the current is actually coming from downstream of the main current flow of where fish gather. So you may end up fishing a swirl hole, backwards.

The best approach for bank fishing a swirl hole is back-bouncing, followed by plunking and drift fishing. Be sure and use enough weight to control your terminal gear.

salmon will either stay holding in the deepest part of the hole, or drop downstream, into the lower section of the deep hole. This is where the bottom actually starts rising and the depth becomes more shallow. Salmon will often hold here as the flowing current which passes over their backs allows them to stay close to the bottom with little effort. This water can be less strain on their bodies as opposed to holding in strong, shifting currents.

Seven-year-old Braxton Haugen battled this chrome chinook in fast holding water. Even in shallow settings, salmon will hold tight to the bottom for a rest.

Swirl holes carry a strong force, and can take your terminal gear away from the sweet-spot without your even knowing it. If you drift fished the upper portion of the hole with two ounces of lead, you may need to switch to four or six ounces to effectively back-bounce the eye of a swirl.

As the day continues, along with the fishing pressure, the

Salmon can be tough to make bite when they drop lower into a deep hole, as they occupy shallower waters, some of which are more clear.

It's worth noting that if the fishing pressure is too great in the upper part of a swirl hole early in the morning, try dropping down to the very bottom at first light. Here you can often catch salmon as

Salmon will travel tight to shore, on the seams of currents and along ledge facings, especially in high water.

they move into the deep hole from downstream. This bite is usually fast, within the first minutes of fishing light. This is because the fish have moved through the night, and now their traveling will slow. Knowing this gives another fishing option for bank anglers.

In the upper part of the hole, early in the morning, start by drift fishing. This allows you to cover the edges and deep part of the current, where fish are holding and trying to move against. When the fish move to the deeper sections of the hole, float-fishing is effective, as is back-bouncing. Back-bouncing is also tough to beat when fishing the lower end of the deep hole. Effectively fishing deep holes for salmon requires that multiple methods be applied. The more versed your tactics, the better your chances of catching fish in deep swirl holes.

Salmon also hold in deep, slow-moving, almost dead, holes. Personally, I've not had stunning success when targeting suspended fish holding in dead water while fishing from the bank. That's not to say it can't be done, rather that the holes I fish are tough to get the proper angle of presentation from where one must stand on the bank. If you do have a good angle to fish these dead, deep holes from, try jigging lures or working a big, wet glob of eggs under a float. Both approaches can be effective. The better biting fish in these dead holes usually hold near the bottom, so don't waste time targeting suspended fish, especially those you can see. Keep the terminal gear a foot or two off the bottom, and you'll be in good shape.

There are some fast-moving, fairly shallow streams that don't have deep holes. Still, salmon must

24 BANK FISHING FOR STEELHEAD & SALMON

rest, and they do this in the middle of fast water; this is especially true for chinook salmon. Where salmon hold is in the slightest of depressions. The fish are looking for a place they can rest, whereby allowing the fast current to scoot over their backs, allowing them to hug the bottom with little effort.

Drift fishing and tossing hardware are effective approaches for bank anglers facing salmon holding in shallow, quick water. It's worth noting that depending on the individual river, these holding spots can change from year to year, as depressions get filled in with sand, rock and other debris.

When targeting salmon like coho and reds, they will hold off to the side of the main currents. For them, depth is not their main refuge, rather slower moving water. Drift fish these slower moving sections, as well as utilize jigs and flies, and

you'll find both coho and red salmon. The same is true of pink salmon.

With salmon, one thing to always watch for is where they are rolling or jumping. Oftentimes, salmon can be seen porpoising in a particular part of a hole. Such action can help reveal the exact place these fish are holding, even show the depth and conditions they're holding in. In holding water, salmon that show themselves on the surface usually equate to there being a bigger school below. Salmon will also surface when on the move. When salmon are observed on the surface, waste no time moving to where they are.

Salmon: Moving Water

When salmon are on the move, they can be a blast to catch. For bank anglers, the decision must be made whether or not to pick a spot and stay there, waiting for moving

When targeting salmon on the move, be ready to offer them a variety of terminal gear.

Subtle, well-thought-out presentations are important when it comes to fooling salmon in low, clear water conditions.

fish to pass by, or to hole-hop, whereby searching for fish as they move through a system. Whatever the decision, the fact is you're targeting fish that are moving. This means it's important to know which type of water salmon move through.

When moving through deep holes, salmon usually pass right on through, and don't bite much. The best places to concentrate your fishing efforts on migrating salmon are in riffles and chutes.

Riffles are a continuous, choppy flow of water defined by the gradient of a stream and the size and number of boulders which make up the bottom. The steeper the gradient and the larger the boulders, the more intense the riffle. If the riffle is too fast and rugged, the fish may move through rather quickly. But if there's enough relief from the current, salmon may take their time getting through riffles.

Some of my best riffle fishing over the years has come early and late in the day, when salmon start

to move. On cloudy, rainy days, I've also done very good in the middle of the day on many types of riffles.

Chutes are another place salmon travel through; chutes are like riffles, but are deeper with fewer boulders in their mid-section. They can be faster moving than riffles, because there aren't the large number of boulders to breakup the current. Still, salmon have no problem swimming up these fast-flowing chutes.

When fishing chutes, spend time hitting the center, where salmon often hug tight to the bottom when passing through. Also, be sure to cover both the inside and outside edges—salmon pull off to the side and rest where the current slows. If these edges are deep enough and offer a consistent flow of water, salmon will also move right up them. When you do catch a fish that's holding on the edge of a chute, carefully mark it, for more salmon will surely follow.

Due to the nature of the fast-moving water in riffles and chutes, drift fishing is the best approach. Just be sure to use enough weight to get your terminal gear on the bottom, as this is where traveling salmon are found in these waters. Lure-fishing can also work well, here. If the target water is close to shore, running a plug downstream is also very effective. This can be done by way of free-spooling it by hand, or running it off a diver and letting it sit in one position, waiting for fish to find it.

Salmon: Low, Clear Water

Catching salmon in low-water situations is not easy. In fact, it's tough. This is because fish are forced to hold in non-traditional waters, which are less protective than what they normally rely on. It's also due to the fact that low water is usually associated with clear water, something salmon are not keen on. Not only can this make it difficult in getting your terminal gear down to where the fish are, but the fish can also be very edgy.

Some of the best places to search for salmon in low-water situations are at the very bottom of deep holes. They'll also move into deeper holes on the sides of streams or main currents, more like where you'd expect to find steelhead holding. All the fish are looking for is a little depth, some steady current flow and a place where surface riffles and trees may break up the sunlight penetration. A steady current flow is important to chinook salmon, as it carries important scents they rely on for navigation. This is good information for bait-anglers to know.

Once you've found where fish are holding, the next step is figuring out how to catch them. Unfortunately, one of the best ways to find salmon in low-water settings is by actually spotting them with polarized glasses. You'll likely scare salmon, as they are far more spooky than steelhead. But when you return there, under the same conditions, you know where the salmon will likely be.

Knowing where salmon are in muddy water is as important as knowing how to fish for them. The author took this big chinook from a dirty, fairly small coastal stream.

Catching low-water salmon from the bank is tough. Because they are so edgy, it's important to make a subtle presentation that won't spook them. That's not easily done

In murky water settings, it's important to use baits that carry good scent so salmon can locate them. Tiffany Haugen did exactly that for this nice salmon.

If approaching these salmon from the side, bobber fishing is still a good approach, and so is drift fishing. When drift fishing, be sure to make presentations smaller in size than what you normally would, so as not to spook the fish.

A more subtle approach that works well in soft, clear water, is free-drifting your terminal gear. Using no weight other than eggs or shrimp, simply cast into a swirl or soft current and let the natural flow of the water carry the bait to where the fish are. It's important to get the proper starting position on the bank with this approach, so the bait can be carried into the target water without spooking fish.

If fish are holding, but not biting, strategically switch out presentations until you find something they like. This may take time, I'm talking hours, but it's worth it. Try different baits, different egg cures, various colors of drift-bobbers, even different styles. Oftentimes, once one fish bites, it will trigger the others to do the same, and the action can heat up surprisingly fast.

Keep in mind that when fishing in low, clear-water situations, any movements you make above the surface are easy for the fish to detect. Avoid quick hand and arm movements that may potentially spook fish. When wading through the water, move slow and quietly. Figure out where you want to go, and get there with stealth. You

from the bank, where long casts and heavy weights are often required to reach the fish.

Nonetheless, there are ways to catch these fish. If approaching them from upstream, try floating a low-profile bobber down to the fish. I like using a small, soft cluster of eggs suspended a few feet off the bottom. This allows scent to be carried downstream, well ahead of the bait, and gets the salmon's nose working. Then, when they see the bait, they're more likely to strike. A smaller bait is preferred as it's less intrusive and less likely to scare fish away in the clear water setting.

may only get a few casts at a pod of clear-water salmon before they spook, so approach with caution and fish them smart.

Salmon: High, Turbid Water

High water is synonymous with good salmon fishing. This is because high water not only offers plenty of places of refuge for fish, as well as safe travel routes and more of them to choose from, but also because the water is normally off-colored when rivers run high. Turbid, murky water means salmon are more approachable and less likely to spook from anglers.

In high-water situations, salmon often hold toward softer edges of the primary waters described earlier. In deep, swirling holes, look for salmon to be on the more relaxed current edges. The edges of swirls and off to the sides of the eyes of swirls are likely places you'll find salmon in high waters. If currents carry into rock walls, fish the faces of these ledges.

Look for boils and work to the sides of those amid deep holes. Boils are created by an upwelling of currents from below, and make it almost impossible for fish to hold in them. Due to this force, salmon will move to the edges of more relaxed currents. Often these edges are surprisingly close to shore, making them ideal for bank anglers to fish.

Where two currents or riffles come together in a high-water situation, focus fishing the V where they meet. This V is usually more relaxed, but still offers plenty of current in which fish hold. Accessing these slots can be a challenge from the bank, so be sure and use plenty of weight to get the gear down. If fish

are traveling through heavy water, these Vs can be real hot-spots. I've had days when fishing high water where fish were crammed into these Vs, and produced exceptional action.

When targeting moving salmon in high water, stay off to the sides of those riffles and chutes. The force of too much water can cause salmon to seek less taxing waters, and these are usually found on inside edges, closer to shore.

The great thing about high-water fishing is the salmon are less spooky. They also seem to be more aggressive biters. Of course, that's not always the case, but has played itself out in this way many times for me over the years.

Because high water is associated with turbid, dirty water, that means smell becomes a very important factor for the salmon angler. In high water, try going to larger baits, as they carry more scent with them. It's also a good idea to apply scents to your presentations, be they eggs, shrimp, drift-bobbers or lures.

These scents lay down a line of smell that's carried downstream. The idea is to have the fish detect these smells, then shift into the line of the scent's travel. Eventually, either the bait will make it to where the fish is, or the fish will follow the scent line up to the bait. Either way, the objective is to get that scent in the water so the salmon has a chance of smelling, then finding your bait. In turbid water, it's important to focus on the salmon's sense of smell because it's more challenging for them to actually see a presentation under these conditions.

Steelhead: Holding Water

Generally speaking, steelhead occupy a wider range of water

types than salmon, and are more aggressive to the bite in most of these settings. The key to successful steelhead fishing is being aware of where they hold and travel, and how

Steelhead hold in a wide range of water, making them a fun challenge for bank anglers to pursue.

With those details in mind, steelhead are capable of living in an array of water types. Their holding water can range from deep holes to extremely shallow riffles. Let's start with the slowest water habitats steelhead hold in and progress to the fast-flowing ones they're known to frequent.

To the surprise of some anglers, steelhead will hold in the bottom of deep, swirling holes, much like salmon. I've caught loads of steelhead in the height of salmon season from these deep holes, on large salmon gear, nonetheless. I've taken them from such holes on clear, warm days, and on cold, windy, cloudy days.

to best fish for them based on where they live.

Steelhead hate sand, and will avoid it at all costs. This is true in deep holes as well as fast water. One of my boyhood dream holes, a place where Dad and I would easily land over 70 steelhead a summer, filled in with sand one winter. We've not caught, let alone seen, a steelhead in there since.

What steelhead do like is fresh, clean-flowing water that won't impede the operation of their gills. Usually, this requirement is easy to find in most streams, that's why steelhead migrate into them each year. One thing to point out, unlike salmon, steelhead do not die upon spawning, however, they do often perish due to the setbacks their bodies suffer from long migrations and the perils of spawning. One report I saw said about 10% of steelhead survive to spawn a second time in their life.

When you find a deep hole that kicks out steelhead, note where you caught the fish. One thing that's for certain about steelhead, where you find one, you'll find others. I've been catching steelhead in some of the exact same spots I caught them 30 years prior, and where my grandfathers and father caught them 20 years prior to that.

One thing I have found when catching deep-water steelhead is that they usually hold on the upper and lower ends of the holes, away from swirling currents. This is likely due to the faster flowing, cleaner water moving through these areas and also to the fact the middle, swirling sections are occupied by salmon.

When targeting steelhead in deep holes, I've seen them move a great distance to strike both baits and jigs. In clear, deep holes, I've seen them travel 13 feet from the bottom to attack a jig. I've also watched them move forward a considerable distance to strike a presentation.

In going after deep-water steelhead, try starting shallow with your presentation, then drop it deeper. This is easy to do when float-fishing, for your depth is simple to regulate. If drift fishing, be sure to start well ahead of where the fish may be laying, so your terminal gear doesn't drift over them.

If, after the first couple of passes you don't get a bite, drop the jig or bait down another foot or two. Keep working in increments, until you find a depth the fish may like. Sometimes steelhead travel a great distance to attack a presentation, other times it has to be right in front of their noses.

Moving in to deep, fast water, the main place to concentrate on is at the upper end of deep holes. These habitats are sometimes overlooked by steelhead anglers as being too fast and too deep to hold

Tiffany Haugen with a dime-bright summer steelhead taken from a section of fairly deep water.

steelhead. Truth is, these areas do hold fish, though not all the time.

Personally, I've had the best results fishing high, fast water when the conditions are clear. I think the fish move out of the slower, deeper holes, and rather than relocating directly in fast, shallow riffles, they hold in the deeper, faster water. When there are large numbers of steelhead in these holes, they can be found throughout it, from one side to the other and in the deep slots in between.

However, the most consistent place to find steelhead in fast, deep water is on the edge of the main current. Steelhead are masters of disguise, and they can blend in with their surroundings amazingly well. For this reason, they'll often pull off to the side of fast, deep holes and stage there, no matter how clear the conditions.

Oftentimes these deep, fast slots can be sight-fished, that is, the steelhead can be spotted, then fished to. Note that current flows can greatly vary from the sides to the middle in deep, fast water, so bring a variety of bank sinkers to use in this situation. Steelhead normally hold tight to the bottom in fast, deep water, so use a set-up that gets the terminal gear in their face.

Classic steelhead water like this will find anglers targeting fish in both holding and traveling water.

Next comes shallow, fast-moving holding water. Shallow steelhead-holding water is perhaps the most classic habitat in which to pursue these fish, and the most exciting. When steelhead are hooked in shallow, fast-moving water, their hard-fighting, tail-walking displays take center stage. Once you tie-in to a big steelhead in fast, shallow water, you'll be hooked on these fish for life.

Steelhead love holding in fast water, usually riffles that take shape below dead water or long, deep holes. As the riffles, even rapids, dissipate the further downstream you move, steelhead still hold in them. Riffles and rapids extending hundreds of yards can hold great numbers of staging steelhead, which is what makes them so attractive to anglers.

But what is it that attracts steelhead, both summer and winter runs, to these holding zones? First is the number of boulders present in this setting. Boulders, combined with the gradient of the stream bed, are what creates the riffles. These boulders and large rocks, in turn, are what create ideal holding zones for steelhead. Think of these large riffles as harboring micro-holding habitats for steelhead, for behind every single rock is a potential holding location for steelhead. Also, the broken surface which riffles and rapids provide diffuse light penetration, making it tough for predators to spot fish; this makes it a safe haven for holding steelhead, no matter how shallow the setting. Some of the best steelhead holding water will range from two to four feet in depth.

Another exciting element to targeting steelhead in fast, shallow water is the fact they can be fished for in so many ways. From drifting bait or jigs beneath a float, to drift fishing along the bottom, to casting hardware and even running plugs from a side-planer, these fish can be caught just about any way steelhead can be fished for. Of course, these environments are among the most fly-fisher friendly, as well.

Off to the side of fast-moving riffles you'll find shallow holding water. These zones are often occupied by steelhead early in morning and late in the day. From what I've concluded, these are fish that have held in fast water all day, or traveled all night, and are looking for a place to relax that's very near the protection of riffles. I also think many of these fish hold in these waters for extended periods of time, moving back and forth between fast riffles in the middle of the river and the soft, shallow edges on either side.

When approaching the edges of riffles, go slow and keep your eyes open for fish. They can often be seen lying only a short distance from shore, sometimes only a few feet. They also hold in surprisingly shallow water, less than a foot at times. If cast to from the right angle—well upstream so as not to spook them—these fish can be very aggressive, too.

Steelhead also hold in slack, shallow water that softly flows through rock gardens. These are good holding zones where steelhead typically congregate after having just shot up through some big, rough water, or have migrated long distances and are simply in need of rest. Subtle presentations are best in these slow, usually clear, slow-water settings.

A final resting place where steelhead love to hold are on slicks. Slicks are located at the head end of a riffle, usually at the bottom of deeper holes and slow-moving water. This habitat offers a relaxing place

A nice steelhead taken from a slick.
Slicks are one of the best places to target holding steelhead.

to hang after making hard pushes through fast, rough water.

A slick is unique in that the bottom drops out quickly, that is, it gets deep, fast as you move upstream. As the water picks up speed coming out of the deeper holes, it creates greater pressure higher in the water column. That means the waters close to the bottom are slower moving, compared to the surface, making it a good place for steelhead to rest with little effort.

Slicks are great for sight-fishing, be it with float set-ups, drifting gear, hardware or even side-planing plugs. Just be careful not to spook these fish before getting a chance to fish for them. Because the water is usually clear on a slick, visibility is good for anglers to spot fish, and vice versa.

However, if you do spook a steelhead on a slick, and they don't move far, the chances of getting them to bite are still very high. At this point it just becomes a game of persistence. Keep trying different presentations until you find one that gets fish to respond. This is where having multiple presentations in your arsenal will pay off...just be patient and learn with each cast.

Steelhead: Moving Water

Catching steelhead in moving water is one of the greatest thrills our sport has to offer. This is where hard-fighting action unfolds, and where anglers realize just how powerful these fish can be.

Rapids and riffles are the primary target waters for moving steelhead. This is because steelhead moving through these zones can be aggressive biters, and they aren't as spooky as when moving through shallow, more clear stretches of water.

In the heavier, deeper waters that make up rapids, steelhead often hold in back-eddies behind specific rocks. This allows them to rest as they make their way through these taxing sections of water.

Mind you, not all steelhead travel at the same rate. Tracking studies have found individual steelhead within a given school vary greatly in how much water they cover. Some fish easily swim over 10 miles a day, while others hold in one spot for

Dissecting a stream and learning where steelhead can be found, will lead to years of successful fishing.

several days, even weeks. Others have been tracked actually dropping downstream considerable distances, so far that they actually leave one stream and enter another. The point is, not all fish behave the same.

However, one thing to keep in mind is that steelhead hold in and travel through similar routes. If you find a steelhead behind one rock in a set of rapids, note the water level and conditions, and always make a cast behind that rock when under similar circumstances. Some of my favorite steelheading hotspots, both for summer and winter fish, are behind specific, individual rocks located in rapid and riffle settings that constitute traveling water.

Be aware of what causes steelhead to move about a section of river, then decide the best way to fish for them. This fish went for a jig right in the middle of a deep, choppy chute.

The same is true when targeting steelhead in fast water. Mark where you catch fish, and repeatedly hit those spots each time you fish. Find the narrow chutes and seams, and work each with pinpoint accuracy. One thing about fishing fast-moving water, it's a game of inches. If your cast is not perfect, the fish may not see it, or the current may be so strong the fish won't go to the effort of leaving their comfort zone to strike at a flashing glimpse of terminal gear.

In more gentle riffles, smaller rocks and a less severe gradient make it more fish, and fisherman, friendly. By that, I mean fish will occupy more locations in riffles because the water isn't as turbulent or moving as strongly as in rapid settings. These waters are also easier for anglers to fish.

In strong rapids, it's important to get your terminal gear down quickly, and control where you want it to go. Due to intense turbulence, not a very high

percentage of rapids can be fished, with most of the best action coming behind rocks and along seams created by these rocks. Riffles, on the other hand, can be fished in a variety of ways. From drift fishing to working jigs beneath a float or casting lures, multiple approaches can be applied in riffles.

Riffles are more shallow than rapid habitats, which also makes them easier for anglers to fish. But just where in a riffle steelhead hold depends on many factors. Impacts such as angler pressure, water temperature, water flow, sun position and more, can impact where steelhead lie in a riffle.

For instance, boat traffic may push steelhead lower into the riffle. It may also force them to the edges of the current, close to shore. Bank anglers, on the other hand, may force fish to move into deeper or more broken water in the middle of the river. Simultaneous bank and boat pressure can cause fish to back down to the lower section of a riffle, are right there. Be sure to cover both holding zones and travel routes when fishing rapids and riffles—the fish can be anywhere.

Steelhead: Low, Clear Water

Some of my best low, clear-water fishing days for steelhead have been spent in deep holes that look more like salmon water. These were during low-water periods where fellow anglers thought the water was so low, steelhead wouldn't be around. There were also those times when river levels were so severely low, anglers concluded there wasn't enough water to draw fish into the system, dismissing it as a poor run-year. Fact is, fish enter rivers as their biological clocks instruct them, and often hold in the bottoms of deep holes rather than moving upstream as they normally would.

Low, clear water can impact where steelhead move and hold. Be aware that where and how you fish low water situations can greatly vary from how you fish high water settings.

or scoot up to the head end. When angler pressure is high, explore all your options.

When the water temperature is cooler than normal, steelhead can pull off to the slower water on the edges of the stream, hold behind larger rocks or drop down low in the riffle. All of these places have slower-moving water, which makes it easier on the fish. Once they do feel a need to move, they can do it quickly, as the faster-moving riffles

The result, anglers don't believe any fish are in the river since they're not moving upstream. Of course, this isn't always the case, but it does happen more often than you may think.

Over the years we've had solid success on winter steelhead when fishing them smack on the bottom of the deepest holes. Here, it's not uncommon for hundreds of fish to congregate in one hole. What draws them there is the protection deep water offers, both in depth and darker color. Summer steelhead can also be found in deep holes during times when water levels are low and temperatures high.

Steelhead also stage in shallow riffles during low, clear conditions. This is because the broken surface offers cover. Many anglers believe summer steelhead in warm waters stage in riffles because the water is more oxygenated. This is not the case. Studies show that oxygen content remains constant throughout the typical Northwest stream, meaning there's no shortage of good breathing water in any portions of the water column.

However, over the years, I've taken a good number of summer and winter steelhead at the mouths of creeks. While these feeder streams don't bring any more oxygen into a stream, what they do introduce is fresh water that can carry different scents than what's in the river. For summer steelhead in warm rivers, these little creeks are often cooler, offering fish a sense of relief. For winter steelhead, the smell of these creeks, especially following a rain or snowmelt, will attract fish.

When fishing the mouths of creeks, don't limit yourself to the mouth, proper. Instead, follow the current downstream to where the incoming creek water is flowing. In faster-moving rivers, this freshet of water can travel close to shore, making for ideal bank fishing access.

One thing to keep in mind when fishing these inlets, if incoming creeks are big, they can deposit a lot of sand at the mouth. This deposition, called an alluvial fan, will force fish away from the mouth, as too much sand is kicked-up, which steelhead won't tolerate. Fish well below these alluvial fans, the cooler

Creek mouths that bring fresh, cool water into a river can be steelhead magnets. Over 20 summer steelhead nosed into this feeder stream.

water will continue downstream. These places often go overlooked by anglers in low water situations.

Steelhead: High, Turbid Water

Unlike salmon fishing, steelheading in high, off-colored water can be off and on. Summer

Oregon guide, Bret Stuart, stuck close to shore to take this steelhead in high, off-colored water.

steelhead, in particular, are finicky in these situations, usually because it means the rivers are on the rise. In these scenarios the bite is usually slow to come.

Winter steelhead are another story, though. Winter steelhead are used to moving in high, dirty streams. Unlike summer steelhead, winter fish are working against the clock. In many situations, when winter steelhead enter a river they don't have long until they start to spawn. While some fish may be in a river a few months prior to spawning, others may be around for only a matter of days before their biological clock tells them it's time to reproduce. Because of this, winter steelhead have no option but to push upstream, often under unfavorable conditions. Where steelhead can usually be found in high-water situations is close to shore. They'll follow shorelines for navigational reasons, and because there's less resistance from water flow.

When fishing winter steelhead in high, turbid water, stick close to shore. More of these fish are caught by plunking— tossing gear out and letting it sit on the bottom—than any other way. The approach is basic, you are simply waiting for the fish to swim by and smell and/or see the presentation.

In high-water settings, winter steelhead are almost continually on the move. This is one of the things that makes going after these fish so frustrating; they often pass by prime fishing holes without so much as seeing a line. But don't wait.

Winter steelhead can be caught in surprisingly murky water. If visibility is about a foot or so, you can catch fish. The key is getting out as soon as the river starts to recover, not once it has recovered. Getting out early will not only put you on the river ahead of other anglers, but it will allow you to catch those fish that would otherwise scoot past. As soon as the rivers start to drop, get after those winter steelhead, fish close to shore and tight to the bottom...you'll be surprised with the results.

One point worth considering, in terms of reading water, is the value of underwater scouting. Because it's so challenging to learn what a river bottom is like from above the surface, try looking at it from below. During hot summer months, hopping in a raft or inner-tube, and floating the rivers you fish can teach you much about how to fish them. Some small coastal streams may even be wadable.

Be sure to take a mask and snorkel along, so you can get a close, clear look at what makes up the river bottom. Look for features that create ideal holding spots or travel routes. See where big rocks are, along with gravel and sandy spots. Take note of where there are hang-ups, and see if you may even be able to get them out of the river. Find ledges and features that create swirling conditions when water levels are higher. This is one of the best ways to truly learn the structure of the river you fish.

In summer I've waded a couple of my favorite winter steelhead streams, doing underwater scouting while setting crawdad traps. The water is usually very low—a good five feet below what it is when fishable—and warmer. This makes it fun for getting out and scouting while simultaneously catching crawdads that congregate in deeper pools. Crawdads are great eating this time of year.

When reading water, approach the task with an open-mind and a willingness to learn. Because so much of what we see on the surface varies from what's actually below, reading water is a skill that takes time and patience to develop. The good part, the more you fish, the more efficient you'll become at reading water, and the more fish you'll continue to catch.

Chapter 3:

The Gear

Since catching my first steelhead in 1968 and my first chinook in 1969, gear, gadgets and techniques have come a long way. Technology has advanced just about every part of our world, and fishing for salmon and steelhead is no exception.

I'm one of those anglers who likes knowing about all the new gear and techniques, but I'm not much of a gadget guy. In other

Anglers have many choices when it comes to figuring out what gear to use on salmon and steelhead.

words, I like using what works, not being loaded down with stuff just because it may look cool. My objective is to get by with as little gear as necessary, and still catch fish.

With that in mind, let's take a look at some of the common tackle needs every bank-fishing salmon and steelhead angler should know. Remember, these are simply basic suggestions to get you going. In this

day and age of specialization, you can definitely invest in more, higher tech' items if it's in your budget.

Rods

You can get inexpensive rods and reels, or you can sink a lot of money into them. Which you choose depends on your personal budget. Based on my years of experience, my suggestion is to buy the best rods and reels you can afford.

Generally speaking, the more expensive a rod and a reel, the better its quality will be, and when battling big salmon and feisty steelhead, you don't want to skimp.

One thing I've been amazed with over the years is how advanced rods and reels have become. These are two items I own a lot of, mainly because they are very specialized, which helps me fish a specific way more efficiently. For instance, if jig-fishing, I want a long, fairly relaxed pole, not my first choice if I were drift fishing.

Let's begin by taking a look at the rods I would suggest considering, based on the style of fishing to be done for salmon and steelhead within most any river setting. For comparison's sake, I'm going to list the rods I fish with, G. Loomis brand, and you can make any crossover correlations to other rod brands based on these styles and descriptions. We'll start with salmon, then cover steelhead rods.

For salmon, be it fall chinook or springers, a versatile rod that's made for bank fishing is important. Bank anglers are often limited on where they can stand, cast and how much they can move to land fish they're fighting. This is why companies go to great lengths to make specialized rods to fit every angler's needs.

When float-fishing for salmon, whether using jigs, bait or both, a good choice gauge is the G. Loomis SAR1084C. This rod is nine feet long, and rated for 10-30-pound-test line and can easily cast up to three ounces. Its oversized guides allow plenty of room for a bobber stop, which makes it great for fishing fall chinook in tidewater, or springers in heavy swirl holes. It's a moderate-action rod, which is something to look for in this style of fishing.

For drift fishing salmon, look for a rod that has a fast action and plenty of power to allow drifting enough weight, as well as back-bouncing. The HSR1023 is an 8'6" rod that handles 12-25-pound-test

How many rods you have depends on how much you want to invest. Today, there are specialized rods to fit every fishing style, in all types of conditions.

line. If targeting bigger fish from shore, step up to something that will handle line in the 15-30-pound class. For this style of fishing, you want a rod with plenty of backbone, as you're fighting fish, trying to maneuver them around obstacles and trying to stay out of the way of fellow anglers.

Spinner-fishing is a technique that's all but become a science in recent years, and with this growth has come the creation of highly specialized rods. Look for specially designed spinner-fishing rods, about 8'6" long and rated for 10-30-pound line. These rods are great for casting

Mike Perusse picked the right gear to handle this Alaska king salmon.

rating of 10-40-pound test is ideal. Longer, stout rods offer a definite advantage over a shorter one, especially in bigger rivers.

If you're not into investing in specialized rods, one of the best choices for an all-around set-up is a nine-footer with a moderate action. This is a rod that will handle up to 30-pound-test line, easily cast two to three ounces of weight, and has enough backbone to handle fish in most situations. It's hard to go wrong with a rod like this.

As with salmon, we'll group the steelhead rods to include both summer- and winter-run fish. These rods also work well for other salmonids, like coho, red, chum and pink salmon.

Float-fishing for steelhead, like spinner-fishing for salmon, has become very specialized. For this style of fishing I like a long rod, one in the 9'6" to 11-foot range. The longer rod allows for very efficient mending of the mainline, which is crucial in controlling the drift. It also has ample backbone for fighting and handling fish.

Another float-fishing rod I like is the longer, 10'6" STR1265C. This rod is powerful, designed for big rivers and big fish. Though it's made for float-fishing, it's one of the best all-around rods there is, working particularly well while drift fishing and plunking. In places where bank anglers have little room to fight fish, a pole like this can make a big difference.

Your best choice for a spinning rod may not be well suited to plunking or drift fishing. There are many options in the world of fishing rods, and it's good to know the design and purpose of each.

lightweight tackle a good distance with stunning accuracy, and their sensitive tips allow you to feel the action of the lure as it works.

Depending on the river being fished, salmon plunkers often cast farther out than steelheaders. They're also battling stronger fish that strive for deeper waters. This means the fights, too, can be carried out over long distances, not to mention the fact hooked salmon often have to be maneuvered over rocks, downed trees and more. For this, a long rod (10'6") with a line

Choosing the right reel to fit the rod and be able to handle the fish you're after, is critical. This setup, with Hydrofloat line and eggs, is ready to float-fish for salmon.

A bit lighter version, the STR1163S is a spinning rod that's 9'8" long but is rated for 8-12 pound test line. It's excellent for both drift fishing and tossing spinners, and has enough power to handle fish all the way up to small chinook, in size.

For specialized spinner fans, the STR1025S is a good model, featuring ample power for big steelhead in heavy water. This two-piece rod is 8'6" long and carries a line rating of 8-17 pounds. This is one of the best all-around steelheading rods a person could ask for. Another great all-around rod is the STR1134C, which is a casting rod that's 9'6" long and can handle 6-12 pound test. This style rod can do it all.

In the past, the trend was for anglers to stick with short rods, between the 8- and 9-foot range.

Today, as technology continues to show its benefits, anglers are seeing the value of fishing with more specialized, longer rods. I think there will be a trend shift in the years to come, and once you start seeing the value of bank fishing with a longer pole, you'll understand why.

Reels

As for fishing reels, this is one of those things that comes down to personal preference and what type of fishing you plan on doing. Whichever route you go, spinning or bait-casting, be sure to get a reel that will hold plenty of line. Remember, bank anglers don't often have the luxury of following hot, running fish up and down the river like boaters do, so be sure to have enough backing.

How you decide to present a certain type of terminal gear has direct bearing on what type of rod and reel you'll want to use.

To figure out which reel is best for you, start with fishing style. That is, figure out which fishing approach you'll be using, and go from there. For salmon, most bank fishing needs can be met with a spinning reel. For steelhead, where more fast water is being fished, it's nice having a bait-casting reel.

A fishing reel should help maximize your overall fishing efficiency, working for you, not against you. Drags should be solid

Selecting the right gear to fit the situation and skill level of the angler is important for bank fishermen.

and smooth, handles should operate with ease and little maintenance. Reels should also be able to cast with ease and take line in with a good gear ratio, that is, few cranks for maximum line retrieval.

For salmon, spinning reels like Shimano's Symetre 4000 or Daiwa's Prodigy 3500 will cover most, if not all, of your bank fishing needs. The Prodigy holds about 150 yards of 17 pound test line, while the Symetre takes about 130 yards, which is plenty for salmon.

If looking for a casting reel for salmon, a larger capacity spool is ideal. Something along the lines of Quantum's 1421MG, has been perfect to meet all my needs.

When it comes to bait-casting reels, try some out in the store. See how they feel in your hand and be sure and test how their drags feel by peeling off some line. I'm right handed, along with about 80% of the world's population, and personally, I prefer a bait-casting

reel with a left-hand retrieve. This is because a stronger hook-set can be had while holding the pole in your stronger, more dominant right hand. More efficient rod handling is done from the cast all the way through to the end of the drift, too, when holding a pole in your dominant hand. Why right-handed anglers use right-handed reels is something I'll never understand. To me, it's like having a right-handed baseball player catch the ball with his right hand, then take off his glove and throw the ball with the same hand. The body's not built that way. Still, I know of many right-handers who love right-handed reels, so see what feels best for you.

When targeting steelhead, I like bait-casting reels when fishing riffles, rapids and fast-moving tailouts. This is because it's necessary to let out line as the terminal gear drifts downstream, so as to cover all the fishable water. For this, a reel along the lines of

BANK FISHING FOR STEELHEAD & SALMON

Shimano's 201 and 251 were, in my opinion, the best reels ever made. Unfortunately, they were discontinued years ago, but they're still my favorite reels to use. A buddy found a bunch on Ebay a few years back, and bought over 20 of them—it was the best money he's ever spent on fishing gear.

If you can't find any of the old 201s and 251s, both left-handed models, look for low-profile reels that like Shimano's Calais, which holds about 110 yards of 10-pound-test line. With the ever-changing, low-profile designs of casting reels and their continuing growth in efficiency, designs are always changing, so take the time to see what feels best to you.

As for steelhead spinning reels, I like having one for float-fishing and another for holding my copolymer line for drift fishing and tossing lures. For float-fishing, where a great deal of floating line runs downstream, I like models like the Symetre 4000. For drift fishing,

If targeting waters with wild fish, going with a heavier line is a good idea. This will ensure fish can be landed quickly, then released, with less stress.

plunking and casting lures, the Symetre 2500, a scaled-down version of the 4000, works great.

How long a reel lasts depends on how well it's cared for. I have some that are still working as well as they did 20 years ago. Be sure to clean them with a gentle spray of warm water at the end of each day. Apply a light coating of grease and only a few drops of oil as needed. Applying too much oil and grease can inhibit a reel's performance, so don't overdo it. Follow your reel's maintenance guidelines as provided by the manufacturer. At the end of each season, be sure to back off the drags on all your reels. This will ensure the springs retain their tension.

Lines

Never has there been such an array of fishing lines to choose from as there are today. What brand,

Finding quality lines that have good strength, low visibility, and a true diameter, are important for salmon and steelhead angling success.

When going after fish in low, clear water, try using a stout fluorocarbon leader rather than downsizing to a thinner, weaker mainline.

style and weight-class line you choose to use depends on the type of fishing you plan on doing. Let's start with salmon then check out steelheading line options.

When drift fishing salmon from the bank, a heavier line than what you'd use from a boat is in order. This is because when you're tied to the bank, you often have to muscle fish into staying in the hole in which you hooked them. If this is not a concern where you fish, then you can get away with lighter line.

For drift fishing, 17- to 20-pound-test line is a good choice for salmon. If working faster, heavier water, go heavier with the line. Keep in mind, the heavier the line, the larger its diameter, the stronger it will be, but also the more resistance it has and the slower it sinks. A thicker-diameter line is also more challenging to cast accurately, and you will also sacrifice some distance.

While on the subject of line

diameter, be aware that there are no diameter police in the fishing world. Any company can make a line of any diameter and call it whatever pound-test they wish. There are general diameter guidelines, but manufacturers don't have to stick to them. When in the store next time, grab three different brands of 10-pound-test line. You'll be amazed at how much they can vary in diameter.

I've used and tested numerous lines, and for the true diameter, abrasion resistance and overall strength, I choose to use Pline for all my fishing needs. I've seen this line do amazing things people wouldn't believe unless they saw it themselves. It's that good. This line runs a true diameter and strength rating.

Salmon are not leader shy like steelhead can be, so you can get away with a heavier line if you choose. Using 40- or 50-pound mainline is not too much for some big fall chinook being fished amid

BANK FISHING FOR STEELHEAD & SALMON

rocky ledges. Going with a 20-pound leader is no overkill, either. How heavy you go, again, depends on where and how you're fishing. I know of some salmon guides who use 70-pound leader to prevent big teeth in big kings from severing it.

I've been most pleased with PLine's CXX Extra Strong line. In extra clear salmon waters, I'll go with moss green colored line, just for the confidence it provides on my end. Their high visibility green as well as their clear lines are good for anglers who like being able to easily see where their line is at, above water.

For steelhead, anything in the 8- to 15-pound class is good for a mainline. Again, which line you choose depends on where and how you're fishing. In soft water with little structure, 8-pound test may suffice. Personally, I never go lighter than 10-pound test mainline, for two reasons: First, if there's a possibility of my catching wild fish that will be released, I want to get them in quickly, revive them and get them back on their way. Second, if there's potential for big fish, I like controlling them, not being controlled, and a heavier line allows that to happen. Twelve-pound test is not overkill on steelhead.

A situation in which heavy line comes in handy is in an area that's heavily fished. In many bank fishing locales where anglers use too light of line, the river bottom is littered with gear and

lines. Some of these lines may be several yards long, a result of being broken off at the rod rather than at the terminal gear. These lines can clutter the bottom to the degree it's nearly impossible to get a good drift. Using heavier line not only prevents break-offs, it allows some of these trash lines to be yanked from the river, allowing the water to be fished appropriately.

When fishing water that's clear as glass, many anglers think they need to downsize their line so it won't spook fish. Rather than downsize and continue using a line with a high reflection rating that

Having the right gear paid off for the author and his five-year-old son, Kazden.

fish can still see, and risk breaking them off, try using a fluorocarbon line instead.

Fluorocarbon has a refraction index nearly identical to water, meaning it's virtually invisible under water. But, as with diameter ratings, there aren't any strict rules on the refraction indexes of fluorocarbons.

What fluorocarbon allows

In the world of salmon and steelhead fishing, matching the right line to your fishing needs is very important.

anglers to do is retain leader strength without having to downsize the line. Fluorocarbon is meant for use in clear water situations. I once fished with a friend in Alaska who insisted we use fluorocarbon in a heavily glaciated salmon stream. I refused because salmon aren't leader shy, and since visibility was only about three feet, that's not what fluorocarbon was designed for.

When float-fishing for steelhead, a specialty line is highly recommended. For years I used a high-visibility floating line, but was not completely happy with its performance as it faded in the sunlight, and the individual strands would break down, absorbing water. They worked, but I wanted something

better. Then I hooked up with the folks at PLine, and we developed a floating line specifically designed for salmon and steelhead fishing.

The line is called Hydrofloat, and is the only line I endorse with my name at the time this book was written. This line floats, has zero stretch, and it lasts. I've gone three years without having to change line, honestly. This line, like braids, is perfect for mending, which is the most important element in successful float-fishing.

For steelhead float-fishing, my favorite weight line is 30-pound Hydrofloat. It has a bit larger diameter than the 20-pound test, therefore floats better in rough, boiling water. Some anglers I've told this to don't get it. "Won't that heavy of a line spook the fish," they ask. No, it won't as it rides on the surface. For chinook, I like the 50-pound Hydrofloat. When float-fishing, I like a strong line that floats well and won't break down.

Terminal Gear

When talking terminal gear, there's no shortage of items to cover. For the purpose of this book, we'll look at the basics. These are must-have items, or ones that have worked well for me over the years.

When fishing from the bank, sinkers play a vital part in which methods you can apply, and how effectively you can fish a specific section of river. In addition, properly matching the sinker to the style of fishing cuts down on hang-ups, increasing overall fishing time.

When preparing for an outing, there are certain measures you can take with sinkers that will improve your overall effectiveness. The easy part, it all starts at home.

If wishing to pour your own sinkers, it's easy. All that's needed is a melting furnace, a few molds and some lead. If you're pouring jigs, hooks are needed.

These days lead is fairly easy to attain. In the past, metal shops sold their scrap lead to private companies, but with ever-tightening EPA regulations, many are forced to unwillingly stockpile the alloy, and they are happy to give it away. Keeping in mind that softer lead yields better quality sinkers, check out local plumbing and sheet metal shops. Lead from these places typically comes in flattened sheets or rolls. Metal dealers, scrap metal companies, roofing businesses and tire shops are also good sources to inquire about getting recycled lead. Typically, lead from tire shops is hard, resulting in brittle sinkers. If possible, mix brittle lead with soft, as soft lead performs better.

Whether you pour your own sinkers or not, knowing which ones to use, when, is critical. For instance, a cannonball sinker will outperform a pyramid sinker when drift fishing or back-bouncing, but for plunking, the pyramid is what you want. If drift fishing a small gravel-bottomed stream, where hang-ups are few yet you want to

Correlating the proper sinker to the approach being applied and water being fished is key to getting that terminal gear where you want it.

keep the presentation down and be able to feel what's going on, then a slinky or caterpillar sinker may be top choices.

The caterpillar sinker is a unique alternative to slinky sinkers, and consists of 1/4" surgical tubing and lead balls. Rather than sealing the lead balls in parachute cord (slinky), they are slipped into surgical tubing. Not only can they be switched out easily, but they can be seen, so you know exactly how many lead balls you are fishing with. The result is precise weight specification, something that can make a big difference when drift fishing small target water.

Sinkers come in many shapes and sizes, and each serves a specific purpose for the bank angler.

There are many styles of driftbobbers. They are one of the most important pieces of gear for the salmon and steelhead angler.

The section of surgical tubing can be as long as needed, typically one to four inches, depending on the depth and speed of water being fished. From one end, slip the lead balls into the tubing and evenly space them apart. The other end of the tubing is attached to the snap portion of a snap swivel.

The beauty of a caterpillar sinker is that it allows for quick changes in weights to meet the needs of the water being fished. With the caterpillar sinker, there is no guessing.

Slinky sinkers (lead shot encased in parachute cord) are another option and can be purchased, ready to go, or made at home. When rigging a slinky sinker, tie the mainline to the same eye the snap is in. Tie the leader to the lone eye of the snap swivel, then run the snap through the cord. This arrangement allows any resistance by the snap and sinker to work against the barrel end of the snap swivel, rather than rubbing against the knot. The result is fewer broken leaders.

Pencil sinkers are another good, universal option. By sliding a half-inch-long piece of 1/4-inch-

diameter surgical tubing up your mainline, then inserting the amount of desired lead, you're ready to go. This set-up is quick and makes for easy change-outs and replacement. It works well in a wide range of waters, especially in shallow streams or deeper, slow-moving waters. It's excellent for drift-fishing steelhead and most salmon. I've caught more steelhead on this sinker set-up than all others, combined.

Bank sinkers (often called teardrop sinkers) are perhaps the best all-around sinker, for they can be used for plunking (instead of pyramid sinkers), free-drifting (instead of cannonball sinkers) and dragging (instead of slinky sinkers). When heading to the river, a range of sizes may be necessary, depending on when and where you fish. Then again, caterpillars or slinky sinkers are also excellent all-around choices, because regulating the amount of weight being used is easily done.

For instance, if fishing fast water where you need more weight, simply clip on two or three caterpillar sinkers, each holding, say, five big pellets. If that's too heavy, pop out a few pellets. The more you experiment with these types of sinkers, the more familiar you'll become with their range of applications.

Not all sinkers feel the same when being fished, and which you choose to use often comes down to personal preference. Figure out which sinker feels best for the type of fishing you'll be doing. Make sure that whichever sinker you use allows you to properly manage your line and "feel" what's going on under water. You should feel every tick of the bottom, be able to detect when it gets pushed or held up by the current, or most importantly, feel when that subtle bite comes.

The sinker is an often overlooked, underutilized tool of specialization, but thanks to ever-changing innovations, it's now easy to find one or two styles that will help meet all your stream-fishing needs. Once you've found the style or styles that fit your fishing

approaches, you'll lighten your load and hopefully catch more fish.

When you know how you'll be fishing, where and for which species, it's time to select the most important part of your terminal gear. The hook set-up is the most important piece of gear that's in the water; it's what the fish will or will not bite. Hooks, yarns, lures, beads, puff balls, drift-bobbers and more, are all items that can be placed on or near the hook for the purpose of eliciting a bite.

Drift-bobbers come in many designs, sizes and colors. They add color, movement and shape to baits. Some also add buoyancy. Some have wings, some are round. Some are painted, others metallic. The variations are many, and they work when fished with bait, as well as fished alone.

Perhaps the most important element in selecting a drift-bobber is matching its size with the hook being used. I don't know how many

When the bite's not happening, try changing out driftbobbers. This steelhead couldn't refuse this presentation.

The purpose of stacking driftbobbers is to give added buoyancy, visibility, color and movement to a presentation.

match the drift-bobber accordingly. If you wish to up-size your drift-bobber, then up-size the hook. This may be the case when arriving at the river and finding it high and off-color. You may want to go with a larger drift-bobber to increase visibility, which is a great idea, just be sure to switch the hook to match. The goal is to achieve more hookups, and taking the time to correlate hook and drift-bobber size is important in attaining this goal. You may only get one bite in a day's fishing—you don't want to blow your chance of hooking the fish because you were using a drift-bobber that was too big for the hook.

riggings I've pulled out of the river over the years, where the hook was too big or small for the drift-bobber. If the drift-bobber is too large for the hook, the fish won't get hooked as the drift-bobber covers too much of the hook point. If the hook is too big for the drift-bobber, the fish may not see it, or see too much of the hook and not strike.

Let the fish you pursue dictate which hook size is to be used, then

Clipping the wing off a winged-dritfbobber can add movement and action fish often find tempting.

Changes often need to take place. If a bait change didn't work try something else, maybe a longer or shorter leader, more weight or fluorocarbon leader. The list goes on. But one of the most basic changes that really can make a difference is with the drift-bobber. It's critical, however, to first understand what drift-bobbers do, before experimenting with them.

Once you know what you want to accomplish by changing drift-bobbers, then you can experiment away. Perhaps the water is off-color. In this case, maybe going to a winged drift-bobber, like a Flashing and Spinning Cheater or Spin-N-Glo, will get the job done. Maybe a darker colored drift-bobber is what you want, to create a silhouette effect which is easier for fish to see. Maybe upsizing a Corky or going to a different-colored presentation is what it takes. It could be you want more lift on your bait, to target semi-

Yarn color can have a big impact on whether or not fish bite. In fact, many anglers use yarn and only yarn, without bait or even a driftbobber.

suspended fish, so go to a larger drift-bobber or thread a couple puff balls onto the hook to elevate that bait higher off the bottom.

I'd suggest investing in a wide-range of colors, sizes and shapes of drift-bobbers...and don't be afraid to use them. You will likely find that some colors and styles work better on one particular river over another.

In addition to experimenting with drift-bobber colors and styles, there's another option that can work well. I've had good success with this approach on both salmon and steelhead, and it has to do with using multiple drift-bobbers, rather than just one.

Stacking drift-bobbers on top of one another not only adds buoyancy, causing the bait to ride a bit higher off the bottom, it also creates more visibility and movement, so the presentation can be more easily seen by fish. The manner in which drift-bobbers can be stacked is only limited by the imagination.

You can stack a pair of the same-size drift-bobbers, say small sizes for steelhead, larger ones for salmon. You can also stack a degree of sizes, say from smaller versions close to the hook, to larger ones on top. Maybe you want a basic drift-bobber on the bottom, a winged version on top. Perhaps a pink one situated beneath an orange one is the color combination you're after.

Whatever the choice, stacking drift-bobbers will work. I've found this approach to be particularly effective on summer and winter steelhead and spring chinook holding and traveling through faster-moving sections of water.

It's worth noting that with the added buoyancy that's gained from using stacked drift-bobbers, there can be a tendency for the top one to ride up the line. It's a good idea to have some toothpicks in your pocket, so you can peg the top drift-bobber so it doesn't ride up the line, whereby leading the fish to strike away from the hook.

There are no limits when stacking drift-bobbers, and the change can produce impressive results. I've spent days on the river where the only thing we could catch both salmon and steelhead on were stacked drift-bobbers. Try it some time, hopefully you'll be just as impressed as I've been.

Another drift-bobber trick includes clipping one wing off the winged-style drift-bobbers like Spin-N-Glos or Flashing and Spinning

There are many sizes, shapes, colors and designs of spinners and lures on the market. Experiment to find what works best in the waters you fish.

Cheaters. I've used the single-wing approach with good results on everything ranging from tiny drift-bobbers for summer steelhead to mid-sized versions for spring and fall chinook, all the way up to giant Alaskan king salmon. Removing the wing from one side of the drift-bobber creates a crippled movement that fish often react to. The uneven spinning is more sporadic than when both wings are intact, and the range of movement is a bit wider.

I have found that when using one-winged drift-bobbers, it's a good idea to stack two to four beads beneath it, so the more intermittent rotation doesn't tangle with yarn or bait tissues. They can also be stacked on top of a smaller, round drift-bobber, like a Corky or Cheater. The combination of more color, exaggerated movement and enhanced motion may

draw a bite when conventional presentations won't.

Yarn colorations are also worth experimenting with. Just as drift-bobber or spinner color can make a difference in drawing a strike, so too, can yarn color. The decision to utilize different yarn colors stems from personal preference, something that's usually developed over time spent on the water. Some people are fanatics about yarn color, others don't give it much thought. However, when you think of such things as water clarity, how fast a presentation moves through a drift, the level of solar penetration, as well as other factors, it becomes evident that yarn color can make a difference in catching fish. In fact, many anglers use only yarn as their color attractant, nothing else.

Knowing what yarn colors work on any given stream, or having the flexibility to change and find out for yourself what works, can make a difference in the number of fish you catch. However, the key is being prepared. If going to a new river, call local tackle shops or sporting

Side planers can increase the number of ways a bank angler can present a range of terminal gear.

BANK FISHING FOR STEELHEAD & SALMON

goods stores to find out what the hot color has been.

I always have an assortment of pre-tied hooks with different yarn colors. I'll typically go with a half-dozen yarn colors on any given trip. This allows me to change colors should one not be working. The color selection can vary, and the more time you spend tinkering with this, the more confident you'll become in using specific yarn colors in different situations.

When steelhead fishing there's a nifty trick you can do to your yarn that will help hook more fish. With the yarn in place, either above the hook or within the egg loop, tie a knot at the tip of each tag end. To do this you'll want to make the tag ends a bit longer than normal, to allow room for your fingers to manipulate the yarn. Then, simply tie a square-knot in both ends.

The purpose of this is so, in theory, when the steelhead bites the bait, the yarn will hang in its mouth just a fraction of a second longer, a result of the knot getting wedged between their pointed little teeth. That valuable moment where the bait spends longer in its mouth can be critical in detecting a bite. It's mind-boggling how quickly a steelhead can grab a bait in fast water, then spit it out without your ever knowing it was there.

When it comes to choosing lures and plugs, the options seem endless, especially when scouring the racks of sporting goods stores. Not many anglers think of plug-fishing from the bank anymore, but that's what plugs were originally designed for years ago, to be cast from shore and retrieved. While this is still an effective approach, the advent of side-planers has allowed anglers to

backtroll plugs downstream, just like boat anglers do. If you spend a lot of time on the bank, these devices are worth looking into.

Lures are one of those specialty subjects on which entire books have been written. Many anglers are now making their own spinners, and catching lots of fish. Many anglers buy a wide range of lures and use them to see what works best. It's a

Knowing what size and color of lure to use is best learned through trial and error. These Pixies are one of the author's favorite spoons when after coho.

good idea to try many sizes, shapes and colors of lures and spinners, and find what works best for your fishing style and the waters in which you use them.

As for color guidelines for lures and plugs, this is a tough one. Many anglers, guides included, will argue these points for days. But the general rule I follow fairly closely is dark hardware on dark days, bright hardware on sunny days. Dark plugs

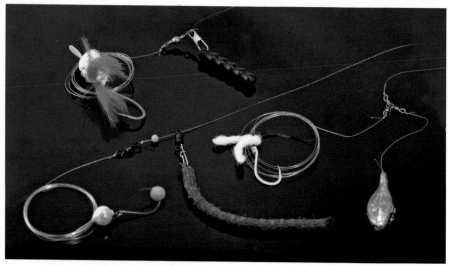

Though small, swivels are an important tool, whereby allowing a variety of different setups to be fished. Here are just three ways sinkers and terminal gear can be rigged.

and lures are proven to create more of a silhouette effect than shiny ones in darker water. This is because the shiny plugs don't have the amount of sunlight needed to flash their colors, and absorb the light rather than reflect it.

It's also worth experimenting with various color combinations on plugs and lures. For whatever reason, call it a confidence thing, my go-to plug in any steelhead river is a 30 or 35 series Hot Shot. I want

Spinner fishing for chinook is almost down to a science in many waters.

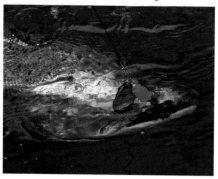

an all-silver body and I'll paint the bill blue or red with a permanent marker. For salmon, my money plug is a metallic silver body and chartreuse tail and/or bill.

For spinners, anglers can experiment with blade and body color and sizes. Some have scent-chambered bodies, others have rattles. Ask around for advice on what works best in the rivers you intend to fish, and start there. But don't get locked into using only what others use. Experiment with size, color and styles, you just may find a secret lure that catches more fish.

The more time you spend on the river, the more aware you become of just how many different types of water are out there and the numerous ways they can be fished. In this age of gear specialization, the ways in which a single hole can be fished have never been greater. There are specialty rods, reels, lines, drift-bobbers and more that can allow a hole to be efficiently covered in various ways. There are also a variety of swivels that can help.

For as long as I can remember, I've been using barrel and three-way swivels for salmon and steelhead. When drift-fishing steelhead, I prefer running a half-inch section of 1/4" surgical tubing up my main-line. Inside this tubing I slide a pencil sinker cut to desired length. The longer the pencil sinker, the more it weighs.

Because the depth and speed of a single steelhead hole can greatly vary from top to bottom, I'll often change-out weights throughout a single hole. When the sinker does get hung-up with this approach, it usually pops out, and the tubing slides over the size-7 barrel swivel, onto the leader. All I have to do to get back to fishing is slide the tubing back above the swivel, then slip a sinker into it.

I also prefer a barrel swivel when using a sliding sinker set-up, as there is less surface area for debris, moss and grass to get hung on as it drifts downstream. These swivels are also good for attaching a snap swivel and sinker to, or running a small dropper from, as when drifting.

Three-way swivels are a good choice when you want some separation among the terminal gear set-up. Anywhere I'm using a dropper measuring a few inches or longer, such as when back-bouncing, plunking or drift fishing, I like using a three-way swivel. The slight separation between the leader and dropper is all it takes to keep them from tangling when being fished. Choosing the right swivel will lead to fewer tangles, less hang-ups and increase your overall fishing time.

When fishing deep, swirling salmon holes, or back-bouncing, even plunking in heavy water with a rocky bottom, there's a device I've been using since the early 1970s that's helped me save hundreds of dollars in potentially lost gear over the years. It's called a spider, and it works like this.

Lead sticks to rocks, resulting in numerous hang-ups and, eventually, lost gear. Spiders are a little cage crafted of stiff wire that surrounds the sinker and keeps it from contacting the bottom by causing it to deflect off rocks. It's not 100% failsafe, it will occasionally wedge between rocks or on a log, but I figure I lose about 1/10 the gear by using spiders.

When crafting spiders I prefer #12, 180-pound-test steel leader. Its pliable yet sturdy construction keeps the sinker active with minimal noise as it bounces over

A spider is nothing more than a stiff, wire cage surrounding a sinker. It dramatically decreases the amount of hang-ups, thus lost gear.

rocks. Cut two 10-inch-long pieces of steel leader. Bend one in half, so a small loop forms at the midpoint. Twist the wire one time to secure the loop, approximately 1/4" in size. Bend the other wire in half and slide it through the loop. Cut a third piece of steel leader, this one about 11 inches long. Fold it in half and place it through the loop so the midway point rests on the bottom of the loop. Now you have six strands of steel leader suspended from one loop.

With a pair of heavy pliers and strong fingers, twist the longest hanging strand of steel around the lower part of the loop and each

Keeping your hook sharp is one of the most important rules in the world of salmon and steelhead fishing.

wire. The other end of the long strand will be bent inward in your final step, and is where the sinker is suspended.

Bend the remaining four strands out at 90-degree angles at the base of the loop. Half way down each leg make another 90-degree bend downward, toward the center. With all fours legs complete, go back and make the sinker-snap attachment.

The snap will be centered beneath and fairly close to the original loop, so it hangs straight

when tied to your line. Be sure to make the snap so you can change sinkers as needed. You now have a four-legged "spider" that should stand alone.

All four legs and the sinker-snap should be firm, not collapsing on themselves at any point. If they tend to collapse at the loop, make another wrap with one of the existing legs. Be certain all legs stay spread equidistant and that nowhere does the sinker hang outside the perimeter of the legs.

The loop made in the first stage of the spider now becomes the point to where you tie your drop line. The mainline is tied to a three-way swivel, and the dropper and leader to the other ends. Sinker centered, all four legs spread, you're ready to fish. I prefer a dropper longer than my leader, sometimes twice as long when fishing deep swirl holes.

Once airborne, the spider and bait separate, just like they do when on the river bottom. Once on the bottom, the spider holds upstream, while the lighter-weight bait travels downstream. Your bait now has the capability of covering a large swath as it's moved around in the current, or shifted about in swirling holes. It's a slick tool I won't hit the river without when going after salmon.

At this point, it's also worth touching on the importance of quality hooks. For salmon and steelhead, you're primarily looking at octopus-style hooks ranging from size 2 all the way up to a 7/0 giant.

Tying good knots equates to catching more fish, like this double.

The bigger the hook, the bigger the target fish. I'll use 7/0 hooks when targeting giant kings on the Kenai River in Alaska, for instance. For most Northwest rivers, a 3/0 hook is fairly standard. This can vary a size or two, depending on the size of fish, time of year and fishing approach being used. Remember one thing, salmon have big mouths with lots of bone; you want a hook that's plenty big and stout enough to handle the big ones.

For steelhead, which hook size to use depends on the river conditions. In low, clear water, a size 2 may be needed. In off-colored water, I'll go all the way to a 2/0, even 3/0 if there are big fish around.

Whichever hook size you choose, be certain they are needle-sharp. Every few casts, check the point of the hook to make sure it's honed. After every hang-up, it's a good idea to check the hook, too. Have a file within

easy reach, and use it. If the point can't be salvaged, tie on a new hook. Many fish are lost, or not even hooked, due to dull hooks. This is one of those things anglers have direct control over, so don't overlook the value of keeping your hooks sharp.

While on the subject of sharp hooks, it's just as important to tie good knots, whether securing hooks, droppers, hardware or mainlines. It sounds basic, but tying solid knots is one of the most overlooked steps in fishing.

A common error in knot tying comes in not properly matching the knot with the purpose of its use. For example, if fishing big fall chinook, where the chances of hooking a 60-pound fish are real, then be certain the knot strength can hold up to the test. At the same time, it's not an overkill to be conservative and go with the highest strength knots that you know will work.

These miscellaneous items take up little space, and are worth toting along on every fishing trip.

Miscellaneous Gear

In addition to terminal gear, bank anglers will want to be sure to have a few other key items with them at all times. Knives, files, needle-nose pliers, scissors and rubber gloves are worth having in possession. Knives can be used for many things, from cutting lines to trimming brush to bleeding and cleaning fish.

Hook files we've already covered, just be sure and use them. Needle-nose pliers are one of the most important tools; they can be used to remove hooks from fish, bend hooks or other gear back into place, cut line, sinkers and much more. They also come in handy in various emergency situations that can arise.

A little pair of scissors can also be handy, especially when cutting yarn, line or baits such as eggs or prawns to desired size. If salmon fishing, rubber gloves are worth having to help keep unwanted scents from contaminating your terminal gear; some anglers use masking soaps or scent-free hand-wipes.

It's also a good idea to have an extra spool of mainline on-hand. If a fish spools you or you develop an unmanageable bird's nest in your reel, it's nice having extra line with which to work. I've seen anglers lose a day of fishing because they didn't have any backup line with them.

If fishing trophy waters, where there's the chance of having a big fish mounted that you also want to release, then bring a little fabric tape measure along. These take up little space, and a quick measurement of the length and girth, along with a couple reference photos, are all a taxidermist needs to preserve your memories in the

Aside from which knot to tie, when working with copolymers and especially fluorocarbons, be sure to wet the line prior to cinching the knot down tight. This can be done with saliva, river water or rain. Wetting the line cuts down on friction which creates heat that can weaken a knot once it's actually snugged down tight against a hook or swivel. The time to wet a knot is when it's still in its loose stage, not once it's been tightened.

Another helpful hint is to make sure there is plenty of tag end on the knot. You don't want it so short that as the line stretches, the tag end is pulled through, unraveling the knot. On the flip side, you don't want it too long to where it catches moss, grass or other debris floating downstream, inhibiting the action of your presentation. Having a tag end that's slightly shorter than 1/4 inch is ideal.

form of a reproduction mount. Don't forget the camera. You may want to put it in a sealable, waterproof bag.

If you're into details, a thermometer can also be of use. Monitoring water temperatures over the course of a day, season or even many seasons, can help you learn a lot about fish.

When fishing waters known to harbor high populations of mosquitoes and other biting insects, you'll want a good repellent that works. The ThermaCELL is one device I've used throughout some of the worst biting-bug areas around the world, including many parts of Alaska. A compact, cordless unit easily straps to a pack or can be placed on the ground. Its butane cartridge burns a deet-free patch that slowly disperses repellent into the air. I like the ThermaCELL because it works and, when fishing with bait, allows me to remain bug-free without the risk of contaminating my gear with liquid or spray repellents. It also increases my fishing time by allowing me to stay on the water.

Wading Gear

For bank anglers, one of the most important pieces of gear is what we choose for wading. In the warmer waters of summer, what we wear will obviously be different than what we wear in the middle of winter. What we wade-fish with in Alaskan waters may also be different from what's worn in the Lower 48.

Rather than highlighting specific pieces of gear, however, let's touch on some approaches of wade fishing and how the gear fits in. In clear-water conditions, pursuing salmon and steelhead can be a bit

like hunting. That is, you're spotting the quarry, then making a move to close the deal. Spot-and-stalk fishing is one of the most rewarding and effective ploys a bank angler can apply.

With drab clothes and quality polarized glasses, you're set. Quiet footwear, like felt soles, can also be beneficial. The next step is to practice stealth. When stalking fish,

When fishing in bug-infested areas, strapping a ThermaCELL to your pack can keep you on the water, catching fish.

assume they will be there, and that it's up to you to spot them before they see you.

Keep a low profile and move quietly, disrupting the water as little as possible. Avoid rolling over big, round river rocks, as this sound carries surprisingly far under water. When searching for fish, try seeking out angles that take the glare off the surface and allow your glasses to penetrate. Look for parts of fish, rather than the whole thing. Oftentimes, all you'll see is the broken outline of something that doesn't match the bottom, maybe a gray, brown or blue line.

Sometimes you'll catch a moving tail, dorsal fin or the silver flash of a steelhead tossing on its side, but the vast majority of the time all you'll see is a faint hint of a fish. When closing in for a cast, be sure to position yourself so you can move in and cast without being seen. Note the sun's position, making certain long shadows from your approaching body do not spook fish. A nervous fish is one that may not bite, and

Clothing, proper wading gear and quality polarized glasses, along with stealth, are important elements when wade fishing.

One of the most important tools a bank angler can have is a dependable wading shoe. This light-weight, felt-bottomed boot crafted by Cabela's is comfortable and reliable.

the objective should be to approach these fish and make the cast without them knowing you're there.

When approaching fish, keeping quiet is very important. Sound travels surprisingly far and fast through water, so be careful and don't be in a rush. If fish are near, the simple task of moving your feet through water should be done with caution. Avoid kicking up water and creating excessive splashing. Such unnatural activity will alert fish to your presence, and either send them on to the next hole or potentially turn them off a bite.

Investing in pair of felt-soled wading boots greatly helps reduce foot noise. If walking on slimy rocks, perhaps the cleat/felt combination sole is the way to go. If on bedrock, a rock that's less noisy to wade on, you'll likely be able to get away with bare spikes on your shoes. I've used old golf and baseball shoes for wading on soft bedrock, and they've worked great, just be sure to walk gingerly when nearing where fish hold.

If you plan on doing much wade fishing, boots with interchangeable soles are a wise investment, they allow you to meet the needs of any bottom type you're fishing. If you're fishing multiple rivers with a wide range of bottom types, these multi-soles can pay for themselves in one road trip. The key to quiet wading is to do what you have to in order to make your way through the river, without sacrificing safety. Often it all starts with a comfortable pair of waders and quality boots.

In cool waters, I like wearing an under layer of athletic-style tights or light-weight sweats. This allows you to fish and move in comfort and eliminates binding at the knees and hips. Personally, I have a few styles of waders to fit the conditions being fished, from warm to cold to extremely cold.

During summer months, steelhead action, as well as daytime temperatures, can be sizzling. In such conditions, it may be worth foregoing the waders and simply wet-wading. I've been wet-wading for summer steelhead ever since I can recall and firmly believe it makes me more mobile this time of year.

For shoe types when wet-wading, felt-soled shoes or sandals work well. If wearing sandals, be sure to get close-toed designs to keep sticks and rocks from poking in. Having some felt on the bottom helps on mossy rocks, too. If wet-wading is not appealing to you, there are light-weight, high-tech waders on the market that work well in hot conditions.

Another valuable wading tool is a walking staff. These are great when wading rough water, or when working through deeper sections to reach a casting station. Just be sure you can get out of wherever the staff allowed you to get into,

The base layer worn under your waders can be nearly as important as the waders themselves, especially if fishing the cold waters of Alaska or Canada.

as currents can change with your angle of approach.

Bait Options

Which baits you choose to use depends on many factors. Time of year, fish being targeted, water clarity and temperature, fishing pressure and more can all play a part in which bait works best for salmon and steelhead.

The egg, or roe, is the most popular natural bait for bank anglers. Be it plunking, drift fishing, back-bouncing or presenting it below a float, eggs can be fished in a variety of ways. Whether curing your own eggs or purchasing already cured roe, be sure to get a clean, blood-free product. You also want one that fits the style of fishing being done.

When wet wading, close-toed sandals are ideal for keeping out rocks and sticks.

The proper egg cure can make all the difference in catching fish or not catching fish.

If fishing gentle water beneath a float, look for moist eggs that are soft to the bite, carry good color and milk-out well. In more rugged water, or where you may be forced to cast long distances, a firm egg is preferred. This is where a long rod can come in handy, to alleviate the amount of whip and pressure a casted bait experiences.

For salmon, a chemically cured egg is best. Look for eggs that have been cured using sodium sulfite, sodium nitrate, sodium bisulfite or similar chemicals. You'll also want to include sugars. Color preservatives, sweets and dyes are essential in concocting the perfect egg cure for salmon.

For steelhead, chemicals are not as important since they are more sight-based biters than salmon, which react more to smell. For this reason, simple borax cures work well on steelhead. There are some borax cures on the market that also have dyes in them which help add color to the cured egg. You can also dye your eggs with Jell-O, powdered Gatorade or Kool-Aid. Sodium-based cures, like those used on salmon, also work on steelhead, but are not necessary. For more on egg cures, refer to my book, *Egg Cures: Proven Recipes & Techniques.*

Prawns and shrimp can also be good salmon and steelhead baits, as can crawdad tails. Tipping your eggs with a bit of these shellfish can also be very effective. Not only does this presentation become more visible, but it delivers more scent into the water. It may also be a different scent than what the fish are used to smelling on other anglers' hooks, and oftentimes that's all that's needed to turn on a bite.

Tipping your egg hook with strips of baitfish can also be very productive. I've caught loads of salmon soon after slipping a 1/2-inch-wide, one-inch-long strip of herring onto my egg hook. When the eggs failed to produce, adding herring helped. The same can be true for anchovies, smelt and other baitfish.

Tuna is another good bait, particularly for salmon. The high oil content of tuna makes it the perfect scent package for fish to find. Be sure to use tuna that's packed in oil, not water, as the scent value is much greater.

I've wrapped plugs with chunks of tuna and caught both salmon and steelhead. Simply remove the tuna from the can, compress the chunks onto the belly of a plug, then secure it with stretchy thread, a specialty thread used for wrapping baits on plugs. This is a quick, simple, effective approach from the bank.

Another option is to use mesh netting designed for tying loose roe into sacs. Tying up several sacs with tuna, they can then be fished many ways. From dangling the sac of tuna off the trailing hook of a plug or lure, to drift fishing it like you would eggs,

Salmon and steelhead have an incredible sense of smell. Applying scents to your terminal gear, even lures, can force a bite when nothing else seems to work.

to suspending it beneath a float, there's virtually no limit to how it can be fished. This is one of the best-kept bait secrets out there.

A section on baits would not be complete without scents. In essence, that's probably the number one goal of baits—at least when it comes to salmon—to introduce scent into the water.

There are also a variety of scents on the market that can play a huge role in your fishing success. Scents are something you need to experiment with to find what works. Sometimes, all that's needed is a change in scent to trigger fish into biting.

Scents come in small, easy-to-handle squeeze bottles or tiny jars that are simple to carry. I place them in my bait box that's tied around my waist, or in the side-pouch of a pack, so I have easy access to them at the same time I bait my hook. If carrying more gear, slip them in a pack. You may want to seal them in a baggy, in case some leakage occurs.

Play around with different scent combinations to see which works best. If fishing eggs, maybe try a herring or crawfish scent. If using tuna as bait, maybe add anise scent. Scents can also be applied to lures, plugs, jigs and more. The technology of sticky pastes and gels allows these scents to stay on hardware through several casts.

You can also make your own scents. Simply blend the ingredients you want and place in a little container to take to the river. Pick up an old blender or food processor, and experiment away. This is not only fun, but highly educational as you start experimenting with different flavors and smells that turn fish on. Take care not to use the same blender for human foods.

Scents are something you need to experiment with to find what works. Sometimes, all that's needed is a change in scent to trigger fish into biting.

BANK FISHING FOR STEELHEAD & SALMON

The author's father, Jerry Haugen, is one of the best salmon and steelhead anglers Scott knows. His attention to details, patience and persistence is what sets him apart from the average angler.

When it comes to bank-fishing salmon and steelhead gear there's a lot out there. Don't be intimidated or overwhelmed. Use the guidelines provided here to get you going in the right direction, and the rest will take care of itself.

If unsure of what to use in the waters you intend on fishing, ask someone. Tackle shops, fellow anglers, even guides can all be of help. When on the water, observe what others are fishing with, and how they're fishing. Pay attention to their gear and how things are set up.

Watch to see which brands of gear they're using, especially if they're catching fish.

There used to be a saying years ago, that 10% of the anglers caught 90% of the salmon and steelhead. I used to believe that, but in recent years this figure has shifted and I think it's due to the introduction of so much specialized gear. Spend time on the water, find what works best for you and always keep an open mind. By trying new gear and different approaches, you will become a more successful angler.

Chapter 4

Techniques & Tips

Now that we've taken a look at the gear required to successfully bank fish for salmon and steelhead, let's look at the techniques. Though general techniques were touched on in Chapter Two, on reading water, now we'll take a detailed look at each specific approach.

How an angler should fish for salmon and steelhead should be decided for them, not by them. By

Drift fishing is one of the most popular bank fishing approaches for both salmon and steelhead. This technique allows you to cover a great deal of water.

that I mean the river being fished and the condition it's in should make the decision on how it should be fished. If you grab your favorite jig rod because that's the way you like to fish, and head to a section of fast-moving riffles to try for steelhead, it may not be your best option to catch fish.

Before leaving home be prepared to fish a certain way, or number of

ways, each of which should fit the requirements of the water being fished. The more versed you are in various techniques, the better angler you'll become, and the more fish you'll catch.

Drift Fishing

Drift fishing for salmon is likely the most popular bank-fishing approach, and it's definitely in the top three approaches for steelheaders. The purpose of drift fishing is to cover stretches of water while keeping the terminal gear close to the bottom. The terminal gear travels downstream at a rate that's less than the natural current flow. This ensures fish will have time to find it, rather than it sweeping by their noses in a blur.

The drift fishing set-up for salmon is simple. My favorite approach is to tie the mainline onto a three-way swivel. Next, tie about a six-inch dropper to another eye. The dropper is what the lead weight will be attached to. On the last eye of the swivel, tie your leader. It's that simple.

This set-up, where the bank sinker is attached to a dropper, allows the bait to freely swing around, whereby allowing natural

Rigs

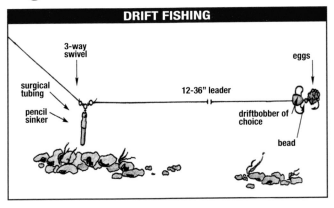

DRIFT FISHING

3-way swivel

surgical tubing

pencil sinker

12-36" leader

eggs

driftbobber of choice

bead

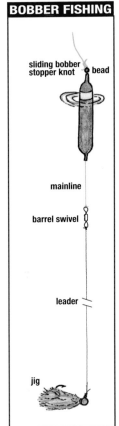

BOBBER FISHING

sliding bobber stopper knot

bead

mainline

barrel swivel

leader

jig

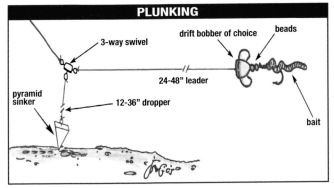

PLUNKING

3-way swivel

drift bobber of choice

beads

24-48" leader

12-36" dropper

pyramid sinker

bait

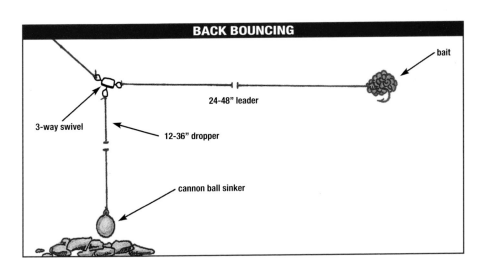

BACK BOUNCING

bait

24-48" leader

3-way swivel

12-36" dropper

cannon ball sinker

The type of water being fished will help determine which rigging should be used.

currents to somewhat guide its direction. If seeking more movement, go with a longer dropper and a longer leader. When drift fishing the bottom end of swirl holes, I'll often have a three-foot dropper and a two-foot leader. When going with a long dropper, try using the spider set-up described earlier to help keep that sinker from hanging in the rocks.

For steelhead, there are a few different drift fishing set-ups to consider. You can certainly use the one outlined for salmon, but go with a shorter dropper. This is because the water that's drift fished for steelhead is more shallow and, generally, not as turbulent as salmon water.

You can also simplify your steelhead drifting set-up. My favorite rigging consists of threading a 1/4-inch-diameter piece of one-inch-long surgical tubing onto my mainline, then tying the line off to one eye of a barrel swivel. The leader will be affixed to the other eye. For weight, simply slide a pencil sinker into the tubing an inch or so above where the mainline ties into the swivel. Be sure and wet the sinker before attempting to slide it into the tubing. This is a quick set-up to make and catches lots of fish.

You can also skip the surgical tubing and go with a caterpillar or slinky sinker. With each of these sinkers, simply tie the leader and mainline into the eyes of a snap swivel. In the snap portion of the swivel that's left hanging, snap in the caterpillar or slinky sinker, and you're set. I like tying my heavier mainline into the eye of the snap swivel to where the snap, itself, is attached. This is because the mainline is heavier than the leader, and will better withstand any abrasions caused by the snap rubbing against it.

Another option is to rig your slinky sinker so it slides up and down your mainline. I've had the best success with this approach when targeting both salmon and steelhead in fairly calm waters. The idea of this set-up is that when a fish picks up the bait in its mouth, it will not feel the resistance of the sinker pulling on the line and drop it. Here, the sinker is able to freely slide up and down the mainline. This is how it works.

Thread the eye end of a snap swivel onto the mainline, then tie the mainline to a barrel swivel. The leader attaches to the other end of the barrel swivel. The snap swivel can slide freely along the mainline. Now, clip the slinky sinker into the snap of the snap swivel and you're set.

The only place I'm not real fond of using this set-up is in fast water. This is because oftentimes the sinker gets hung up, and you may not realize it. Rather than quitting the drift, time is wasted feeding more line downstream, letting the terminal gear float its way through the water. Thing is, it's not weighted down, so it floats too high in the water column, thus wasting valued time and potentially spooking fish. Still, it has good applications in the right situation.

When drift fishing with any of the set-ups described, be sure to cast upstream at an angle that allows your terminal gear to naturally drift into the target water. Keep in mind that the target spot may be up to 20 yards or more downstream from where your cast hit the water. If the gear didn't make it into the sweet-spot, reposition the next cast to try and make it drift to where you want it. Sometimes, hitting the target may

require a change in your physical position in order to find the right current to carry your gear to where you want it.

The best drift fishermen I know are the ones who approach this strategy with a well-thought-out plan. They don't just get to the river and start casting. Instead, they systematically place each cast with precision, picking apart every bit of fishable water. Typically, start by covering the water closest to the shore you're fishing from, as this will decrease the chance of spooking fish by having a line pass over them. This is true for both salmon and steelhead.

The following cast should be a foot or so farther into the stream, and so on with each subsequent cast. Granted, drift fishing for

Hitting your target water is one of the keys of successful drift fishing. This fish fell for eggs drifted under a float.

steelhead requires a great deal more water be covered, because steelhead hold in and travel through more water types than salmon. Still, even on salmon, approach it systematically.

Once you've covered the water from that spot, drop downstream five to ten feet and do it all over again. The objective is to cover every bit of fishable water. Some stretches may take half a day to

A systematic approach can yield good results to the willing, patient angler.

cover, others only a few minute, it all depends on the river being fished and the fish being targeted.

If drift fishing spinners or lures, the grid-casting approach is the same. The only difference, usually you're fishing with just the lure attached to your line. Sometimes a lighter leader may be preferred, which is easily attached with a barrel swivel. Small sinkers can also

be used to get lighter-weight lures down deeper.

Float-Fishing

Bobber-and-bait fishing for salmon and steelhead continues to grow in popularity. The great thing about this approach is that it's the easiest form of salmon and steelhead fishing to master. It's also fun. I don't care how old the angler, no one gets tired of watching a bobber, anticipating when the strike will come...though not everyone may admit it.

Fishing with a float for salmon and steelhead has many advantages. Two of these advantages stand out above the others, and those are the facts that this approach allows so much water to be covered, plus it allows water to be fished that may normally go overlooked.

Typically, when float-fishing—if the conditions call for it—a cast can be made directly upstream, allowing you to fish water that would find you getting hung-up if drift fishing or tossing spinners in that same direction. Once the terminal gear hits the water, flip the bail and take-up the slack as the float approaches you. This allows water to be fished that may otherwise not be reachable, or better yet, reach it from a vantage point that alleviates the concern of spooking fish by wading the shoreline.

As the float drifts past you, simply open the bail and free-spool the line, letting the natural current take the terminal gear downstream. The objective is to achieve a relaxed presentation as the terminal gear moves with the current.

The first couple of casts are most important, as this is when to determine the depth at which you should be fishing. Ideally, when fishing bait for salmon beneath a float, you want the bait close to the bottom, where these fish hold. Try getting it within a foot of the bottom. For steelhead and more aggressive coho getting it within a foot or two off the bottom works well. I've had both of these fish travel great distances, over 10 feet, to attack both bait and jigs presented under a float.

Once it starts drifting, if the top of the float tips downstream, then the leader is too long and the bait is hitting bottom. To remedy this, simply shorten the depth of your bobber stop, or leader, depending on which set-up is being used. If the top of the bobber tips upstream as it floats, then the mainline is likely creating too much drag and is in need of proper mending.

Another great advantage of float-fishing is that it's simple to master. No matter what your level of fishing experience, anyone can quickly catch on to float-fishing. This is also a very subtle approach, which means spooky fish can often be fished from well upstream. Covering water 75 yards or more downstream from where you're standing is easy, as long as conditions allow. Multiple baits can be offered under a float, which we'll touch on in a bit.

One of the keys in covering so much water while float-fishing is the mainline. I know of many great float anglers who like their copolymer and braided lines, and regularly catch fish. Personally, it was the copoly's that drove me crazy during the early days of my float-fishing, back in the late 1980s. My biggest struggle back then was lack of line control.

One of the aspects of float-fishing that catches beginners by surprise is how aggressive the

Float-fishing is one of the fastest growing, and most effective, ways to catch salmon and steelhead from the bank.

A long rod not only helps in mending the line when float-fishing, it also aids anglers during the fight by displacing direct pressure exerted by the fish.

mending process is. As in fly-fishing, the mend is when you lift your rod tip to pick up the line off the water's surface, then set it back down on the upstream side of your terminal gear. This results in a drag-free, natural drift.

Because float-fishing lines don't have the diameter or buoyancy of fly lines, mending is much more assertive. The more choppy the water being fished, the more pronounced the mend will be. This is especially true when fishing great distances downstream or across a current, where more effort is often required to lift the mainline off the surface of the water in order to prevent the current from carrying it ahead of the terminal gear. This usually results in an unnatural presentation.

An aggressive mend can find you reeling in several feet of line, then quickly jerking the rod tip, upstream. This may result in

skipping the float across the river's surface, even sending it airborne. That's okay, since the primary goal is to get the terminal gear, float and mainline all heading downstream at the same pace in order to achieve a natural rate of presentation. While this exaggerated movement may pull your gear off-course, that's okay, the drift can be resumed at any point.

Being able to anticipate what the terminal gear is going to do based on the action of the floating mainline, you'll be better prepared to make mends as needed. Mends made on artificial presentations can be more aggressive than with baits, for the simple reason the harder you jerk to mend the line, the more susceptible a bait is to falling off. This is where using the right bait for the right situation will help increase your overall effectiveness.

Float-fishing with a longer rod than what you'd use for drift-fishing is helpful, especially when it comes to mending. Try something in that 10-foot range. Whatever your rod choice, make sure it has ample backbone so mends can easily be made in heavy water.

When float-fishing, spinning reels are the best way to go. The take-up and let-out rate is much quicker with these reels—versus bait-casters—so your overall efficiency is maximized.

There are various ways to rig a float-fishing set-up, and my favorite is an approach I've now used for over a decade. Onto my mainline, I'll slide a bobber stop (nylon nail-knot), followed by a 3mm bead, then a West Coast Float. The bobber stop is your depth regulator that, when snugged tight, won't slip up and down the line. The bead simply keeps the bobber stop from passing through the float as the terminal gear sinks. Tie the mainline to a barrel swivel, and you're set.

Which barrel-swivel size you use depends on the fish you're after. Size 7 is a good overall choice, though you may need to go bigger if targeting trophy-class kings. In big water, or if fishing swirling conditions, attach an in-line sinker to the bottom eye of the barrel swivel. The purpose of the weight

is to make sure the bait sinks, rather than getting haphazardly tossed around in the current. If running a longer leader, say three feet or more, it may be necessary to position the in-line sinker midway down your leader. To do this, simply cut the leader in two, then reconnect it with the in-line sinker.

In lighter or calm water where bait is fished it might not be necessary to add one or two ounces of lead. In this case, simply attach the appropriate number and size of split-shots to ensure the bait sinks.

Another sinker option is to take

Float-fishing is effective on all salmonid species. This pink salmon, taken by Sharon Manente, couldn't resist an Over The Edge Jig.

a half-inch-long piece of 1/4-inch surgical tubing and thread that onto your leader before tying it to the swivel. Now all you have to do is snip a desired length of 1/4-inch pencil sinker, slide it into the tubing and you have an instant sinker. What's great about this set-up is you are free to position the tubing and sinker where you want it on the leader.

If fishing jigs, whether tiny 1/32-ounce or heftier 1-ounce, chances are you won't need any added weight, as the lead jig heads serve the purpose of getting the jigs down. As a rule of thumb, it's a good idea to match the weight of the terminal gear with the weight of the float. For instance, if fishing an 1/8-ounce jig, use an 1/8-ounce float. If using a cluster of eggs with a 2-ounce in-line sinker, use a 3-ounce float. Listed float weights tell how much weight they are capable of supporting, not necessarily how much they weigh.

Now that the rod, reel, float and terminal gear set-up are in place, it's time to hit the river. Keep in mind that because float-fishing is so popular, specific techniques for this approach are always advancing. That said, the more you learn about float-fishing, the more you want to experiment with different set-ups to see which works best for you.

One such approach is bobber-dogging, a term derived from boon-dogging, or more properly, boom-dogging. Bobber-dogging is an approach where a bank angler casts out his gear, then walks downstream with the presentation. In long stretches of water, a few hundred yards can be covered in this way as the bobber keeps the gear from getting hung-up. Just make sure you're not infringing on fellow anglers, as this approach covers great distances.

As with all forms of fishing, success comes down to being able

Plunking is highly effective in high, off-colored waters like this.

BANK FISHING FOR STEELHEAD & SALMON

One of the most effective approaches when it comes to catching winter steelhead is simple plunking.

to read the water and knowing where the fish are, then getting the terminal gear where it needs to be. The great thing about float-fishing is that it's the most universal approach there is. You can get a float set-up into plugging or back-trolling water. It also works in shallow spinner or fly-fishing situations. Deep swirls, back-eddies and side currents all can be fished with a float set-up. Even frog water can be effectively fished with a float and bait or jig.

Want to try something other than a jig, pink plastic worm, eggs, shrimp, sardines or herring chunks beneath the float? Then tie on a small spinner with a light-weight, sensitive blade and run that through choppy water. You may be surprised with the results.

The more time you spend fishing with floats, the more you'll learn. What you'll discover is there are few limitations on how and where a float

set-up can be fished and, in the end, that's the beauty of this wonderful, very diverse approach.

Plunking

For winter steelhead anglers, plunking could well be the most widely used bank-fishing approach there is. Salmon anglers apply this technique to a large degree, for all species of salmon. As with float-fishing, this approach is simple to master and is very effective. Though the level of anticipation isn't quite what it is with watching a bobber, it's still fun.

The plunking set-up is simple. As with the drift-fishing set-up, tie the mainline to a three-way swivel. It's worth pointing out that because plunking is usually done in high water situations, you can go with a heavier mainline. This is ideal for helping to keep fighting fish out of the brush, as it allows you to apply more pressure on them.

Mike Perusse and the author double-teamed this pair of hefty steelhead. These two anglers have spent many years on the water, learning how to catch fish.

With the mainline tied to one eye of the swivel, tie a dropper to another eye. The dropper should be about a foot long, with a pyramid weight tied at the opposite end. Be sure to use enough weight to keep the gear in place. A leader of two to five feet in length can be used, depending on the fish being targeted and the speed and depth of water being fished. If your target slot is narrow, go with a shorter leader. If you want the leader to move around a bit and cover water, lengthen it out.

Many plunkers prefer a pyramid sinker because it holds the terminal gear in one place. Other anglers opt for a cannonball sinker which allows the bait to move around the bottom a bit. The flat, coin-shaped sinkers called disc sinkers are also good for plunking. Disc sinkers lay flat on the bottom and hold well in strong currents.

Just about any type of bait or artificial lure can be fished on a plunking rig. From baits to bare drift-bobbers, spinners to plugs and more, they can all be fished by way of plunking. A favorite piece of terminal plunking gear is nothing more than a Spin-N-Glo, no bait. The moving action of this drift-bobber is especially attractive to fish, and it's easy for them to find in high, turbid water.

A Luhr Jensen Jumbo Jet Diver can also be used in place of a sinker when plunking close to shore, as this will keep the bait in one place at the target depth. The big-model diver is preferred as it stays down and keeps its course. The diver works well when fishing only a short distance from shore, where it has a seam or current line in which to maintain its direction.

Typically, because plunking is a high-water approach, keeping terminal gear near shore where migrating salmon and steelhead travel is best. There are situations, however, where plunking takes place further into the river. Keep in mind, the further you cast out, the harder it becomes to fight the current and keep your plunking gear where you want it.

Know that fish traveling in high water normally hug the inside corners of bends in the rivers, so casts are normally kept close to shore. Fish will also scoot along main currents that swing close to shore. The plunker is normally targeting fish on the move, so focus on the traveling water, not holding water.

Plunking is a game of patience, and relaxation. It's not uncommon to see several anglers gathered at one hole, rods stuck in holders that are driven into the ground, awaiting the bite. Gathering around a fire, stories can be told and knowledge shared. That's one of the joys of plunking.

If you've never plunked—often referred to as anchor fishing since you're anchoring your gear on the bottom—be patient. In this style of fishing you're waiting for fish to come to you. It's a passive technique, but one where little gear is lost, and loads of fish can be caught.

What I like best about plunking is that it's perhaps the best high-water technique. Plunking allows you to be fishing days before anglers using other techniques.

With so much gear to choose from, and so many ways to fish, try letting the river decide your best approach for catching fish. Study the water. Look at the currents, seams, slack-water spots, back eddies, swirls, holding zones and other waters you think should be fished, then deduce which techniques are best suited for the situation.

Keep in mind, the best way to learn is by spending time on the river, actually fishing. Sure, you'll make mistakes, but as long as you learn from them, that's all that matters. I make mistakes every time out, and were it not for that, I wouldn't hold the level of appreciation that I do for this great sport. I also wouldn't continue learning, which is what I truly love about fishing for salmon and steelhead. No one has it all figured out.

Chapter 5

Smart Bank Fishing

Bank fishing presents many options. Whether it's gear or techniques, places to go or strategies, there are many ways to go about bank fishing for salmon and steelhead.

Since we've covered what's needed to help you become a successful bank angler, let's take it one step further. In this chapter we'll take a detailed look at specific elements related to bank fishing that, if taken into consideration and applied at the right time, can dramatically increase your catch rates.

Stay or Go?

Bank anglers have two options: stay put and wait for fish to come to them, or keep on the move, searching for fish. Which option you choose depends on many factors, not the least of which are water levels, bank access, fishing pressure, weather conditions, run timings and much more.

Unless you're spending the day at a single hole waiting for fish to arrive, one of the biggest detriments a bank angler can have is being tied down. If you're not mobile enough to find fish, it can be tough catching them. Being mobile relates to many factors, from which gear you bring to water levels to how much time you have to fish.

Oftentimes, bank anglers hit one or two spots before work, so don't have much time to devote to finding fish. Still, if you're not catching fish, and other anglers around you aren't catching fish, it may be in your best interest to move and search for them. That not only goes for one particular river or section of river, but for exploring other rivers as well. One day a buddy and I hit three different rivers before we found fish.

Having the right gear to fit your fishing needs can have a huge outcome in your overall fishing success.

Having kept track over the years, I've found that the majority of fish I've caught from the bank, especially steelhead, have come in the first 15 minutes or so after my initial cast. This is usually the result of the fish being in the hole, then my showing up and offering them something they liked.

As for salmon, some of my best bank-fishing results have come by being mobile enough to move within the same hole. Some of the classic salmon holes bank anglers can reach are large, often characterized by a riffle at the upper end, ledges below that and big swirl holes at the bottom. This means salmon can occupy a variety of places within one large hole and oftentimes it takes moving around that hole and trying different approaches to find them.

When traveling in search of fish, bring only the gear you need, no more. However, be ready to fish a different method should the need arise. You may be floating jigs at one hole, drift-fishing eggs at another. Diversify, be willing to try various approaches and stay on the move. Equipping yourself to be mobile can pay off in the form of more fish.

Avoid toting those big tackle boxes and coolers along. Also, leave the net at home and tail your catch. I can count on one hand the number of steelhead I've ever netted from the bank, and not that many more salmon either, other than when fishing in deep holes.

If traveling light, often all you need are the pouches in your waders to carry the gear.

Tailing fish is easy. Get them tired, lift the rod to get their head on the surface, then coast them toward shore. Then, move in behind and grab the base of their tail. Continue walking to shore, rod tip held high, keeping pressure on the fish, and that's it. Not having to carry nets makes it easier to move, and tailing's an effective way to land fish, too.

When bank fishing, try leaving your net at home so it doesn't tie you down to one spot...with a bit of practice, tailing your fish is easy and effective.

The Haugen boys enjoying a fun day on the river.

As the sun breaks over the mountains about 10:00 a.m., the fish move in to the riffles. As the day passes by, boat traffic pushes them over to one section of the channel. At the same time, if fish are on the move, they are continually funneling through the hole. In this situation, it's best to stay put and keep casting to different places within the same stretch of water.

At one of my long-time favorite salmon holes, the fish are almost always there early in the morning, but oftentimes the bite doesn't turn on right away. Sometimes the bite comes around 7:00 a.m., other times not until 11:00. One never knows. But if the fish are in the hole, there's no sense in moving because once a salmon bite turns on it can trigger a chain reaction, and just that quickly everyone is catching fish.

Evaluate the situation at hand. Find the best place to stay near a specific hole and stick with it. Keep optimism high, always believing that the next cast could be the one to produce fish. The only time you may want to move from such a hole is if no fish are showing or you're not feeling them with your line. Sticking to one hole can have its rewards, as the bite can come fast, making it worth the wait. Then again, if you feel the need to move, go for it.

Now, if you want to stay put and wait for the fish to come to you, that's fine. It may be that where you bank fish all you have to do is simply wait for the bite to turn on. No single rule applies to every situation, so it's important to assess the whole picture before making a decision on whether to hole-hop or stay put.

In one of my favorite summer steelheading spots, a person can spend the entire day there, waiting for fish to arrive. Early in the morning, fish are spread out. They'll be on slicks, as well as in the lower end of the deeper holes. They'll also be making their way into the lowest riffles.

Sight-Fishing Steelhead

When bank fishing for steelhead, there is a specialized technique worth highlighting that is rarely applied on salmon. Sight-fishing allows anglers to find fish, then figure out the best way to catch them.

Locating steelhead, offering them a presentation they can't refuse, then watching them gobble the attractant is a thrilling sequence. But this style requires diligence in order to find consistent success.

Anglers intent on sight-fishing for steelhead must take an offensive approach. That is, a strategy must be well orchestrated prior to wading into a stream, finding a fish, then convincing it to strike. Oftentimes the search for fish begins 100 yards or more from the stream, depending on the surrounding topography. The more quickly fish can be seen, the less likely the chance of spooking them.

Steelhead have excellent sight when it comes to viewing objects out of the water. For this reason it's imperative anglers try and locate fish from a safe distance. Expect fish to be in the hole, don't hope for them to be there. By knowing fish are holding in an area, you're more apt to slow your approach and more thoroughly search the section of water for steelhead.

A controlled approach is critical, and that's why it's advantageous to spot fish from afar. Elevated hillsides overlooking a stream, trees, bridges, even a friend's shoulders can offer vantage points by which to more easily spot fish. Some steelheaders are toting ladders to their favorite bank-fishing holes, using their elevated positioning to gain a better viewing angle into the water, and with good success.

By putting yourself in control of the situation from the outset,

In sight fishing, take an offensive approach and move with caution, making sure to position yourself wisely. Elevated places, like bridges, are excellent platforms from which to spot fish.

Quality polarized glasses are a must for effective sight fishing.

your chances of catching fish dramatically increases. This means getting as close to the fish as possible without spooking them, before making the first cast.

Not always do fish hold in water where they are easy to see. This shot shows how valuable it can be to find an elevated position for spotting fish.

If fish are stacked in a stretch of river, put yourself in the best place to maximize catching the highest number of fish from that area. Start working the school from either the upper or lower end, trying to keep any hooked fish away from the largest part of the school.

For anglers new to sight-fishing for steelhead, it can be a frustrating experience until you learn what you're looking for. Rarely will an entire bright-sided, blue-backed fish be seen. Instead, it's parts of fish that will be discerned. Perhaps the twitch of a tail or the outline of a back will catch the eye, which can make the game appear deceivingly easy.

More times than not, these masters of disguise are located by searching for color variations that set them apart from their surroundings, rather than attempting to locate a clear image of an entire fish. In clear stream settings, look for blue, brown, gray and light green hues that differentiate a steelhead's back from the river bottom. Often these

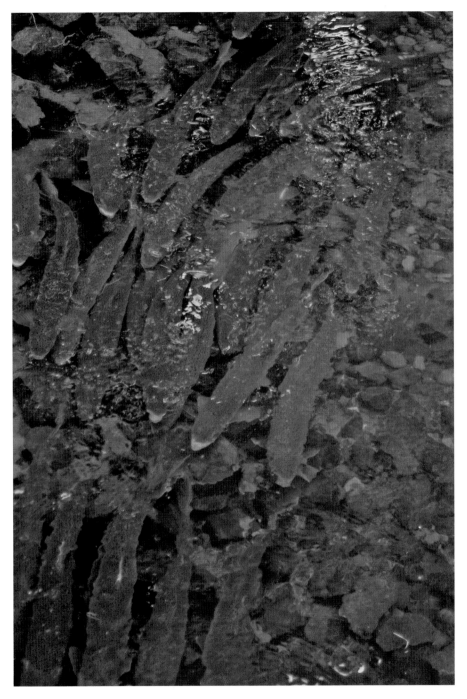

Though holding in a nonfishable raceway, the white mouths of these steelhead are clearly evident from above. Looking for this in fishing situations has helped the author catch many fish over the years.

differences are subtle, and are overlooked by anglers.

I once watched a father and son team wade along a stream in search of steelhead. They beat me to one of my favorite holes where they proceeded to cast into the middle of the stream for the next 30 minutes. Patiently, I sat on the sidelines until they were done.

"No fish in there," they remarked as we passed one another. Four casts later I had two steelhead.

The anglers were casting beyond the steelhead, as they failed to see the fish laying 15 feet from where they stood. Granted, in the broken riffle it was difficult to see the fish, but I managed to land two of the three steelhead that were holding there.

Practice and a quality pair of polarized glasses are the two most important ingredients when it comes to spotting fish. When first learning to spot fish, try and identify them from a distance, keeping an eye on what you believe to be a fish while approaching closely enough to confirm the sighting. Many fish spook when approached in this way, but it's a valuable crash-course in sighting steelhead, and saves many hours of guessing what object it is you're casting to. The more practice one can gain in locating and verifying that what they see is a steelhead, the quicker they will develop the skills of sight-fishing.

A good pair of spotting glasses is a must when sight-fishing. The key is finding a quality pair of glasses that fit snug to the face, blocking out incoming solar rays from all sides, while at the same time allowing ample breathing room. I once had a pair of shades that fogged so frequently they made it tough to fish. Each time I wiped the fogged lenses, they smeared to the point clarity was drastically

When you catch a steelhead, mark where it came from. Chances are more will be there, soon.

When fishing on private land, take care not to litter. Treat the land as if it were your own, and remember, you're representing all anglers.

minimized. Though these glasses were quite pricey, I couldn't replace them fast enough.

Amber, gray and copper colored lenses work well to meet the lighting conditions encountered in most Northwest waters. When sky conditions vary, I'll often carry along three pairs of glasses with different tinted lenses, enhancing my fish-sighting capability throughout the day.

When spotting steelhead in dark-colored streams, try working into position from the upstream side. Steelhead have white mouths, and as they pump water through their system for needed oxygen, their movements are often accentuated in darker waters. Their white mouths set against a dark backdrop can often be dead giveaways as to their presence. Also, because fish can be so closely approached in dark waters, catching

a glimpse of a silver side of flashy gill plate is common.

There are several ways to catch a fish you've sighted. These fish can also teach a great deal about how finicky they can be, making you realize that a lot goes on under water where we can't see the fish. Once you drift a half-dozen presentations over a fish for a solid 30 minutes, and it doesn't so much as look at your bait or budge from its position, you'll be humbled at how challenging it can be to catch these fish.

With that in mind, however, I'm a firm believer that if you've spotted a fish, made a few casts to it and it hasn't moved, there's a high chance of catching that fish. The keys to catching these fish are persistence and change. Persistence equates to not giving up, no matter how frustrating the situation becomes. Change comes in the form

Pitching a tent is not only fun, but it removes you from crowds. Such efforts are often rewarded in the form of more fish, and a peaceful experience.

of altering your offerings every few casts. You may also need to change your method of fishing.

Fishing techniques for catching fish you've spotted are not much different than when fishing blind, to fish you can't see prior to casting. Casting lures has yielded above average results for me over the years. Floating jigs and bait under a float by these fish has also produced fairly consistent results, as has drifting bait. Drifting various drift-bobbers by them, without any bait, can also produce a strike. But perhaps the most effective approach has been anchoring a bait smack on the nose of holding fish.

Basically, what this approach equates to is plunking for the fish; it's just that you've spotted the fish and know where it's at, and know where your cast must end up. It's also a bit different from true plunking because you're targeting

a holding fish, rather than awaiting the arrival of fish on the move.

When sight-plunking, use your drift-fishing set-up. The only difference is rather than a 1/4-ounce weight, attach two to three ounces. Because sight-fishing is usually a shallow-water approach, light weight is the normal protocol. But because you know the fish is holding in normally fast-moving water, the objective is to stop the bait right in front of it. This can only be accomplished with heavy weight.

The idea is to trigger the steelhead into biting by frustrating it. Steelhead are very temperamental, and don't like objects invading their space. Parking a bait on its nose can make that bite happen. If the fish doesn't bite on eggs, switch to shrimp. If that doesn't work, try a different-colored drift-bobber, minus the bait.

If that doesn't work, try a couple beads on a size-2 hook. If that fails, try a Spin-N-Glo covered with a scent you've not yet tried.

Keep changing your presentation until you find what triggers a bite. As long as the fish stays in sight, it can usually be caught. Once it spooks out of the hole, it's game over.

One last word on the subject: Keep track of where you spotted the fish and the conditions at the time. Chances are very high that more fish will hold in the same spot, making it easy for you to spot them the next time through. Though sight-fishing is a challenge, it's also a great learning tool for seeing how fish react to angler pressure. There's no doubt in my mind that sight-fishing has made me a much better angler. It will do the same for you.

Increasing Access

One of the biggest challenges for bank anglers is finding a place to fish. For newcomers, driving roads that parallel rivers, looking for a conglomeration of parked cars and following the footpaths down to the river is about all the where-to directions needed for them to get started.

On the other hand, if looking to gain access to private property, start early and play by the rules. Trespassing is against the law, so make certain you have permission to be on private land before setting foot on it. Also, remember the fact that you are representing all anglers when on the river, be it on public or private land.

One of the best stretches of springer and summer steelhead bank-fishing water I grew up fishing was recently closed-off by landowners. I, like many anglers in the area, had been fishing this spot for decades. But the landowners finally got tired of anglers walking where they didn't have permission to be and leaving trash strewn about the property. Not only were Styrofoam sandshrimp cartons left all over the banks of the river, but so were beer cans, bottles, line and more. The fact these same people—I hesitate to reference them as anglers, since they were so disrespectful—chose to use the property owner's land as a bathroom was the final straw. Just like that, the landowner had no choice but to close off all access to anglers. I would have done the same thing.

Noted Alaskan, full-time guide, Greg Brush, takes many clients each year whose intent it is to learn something specific about salmon and steelhead fishing.

Some of my best fishing experiences in Alaska have come where we hiked, camped, fished, and kept hiking the next day. This allows you to distance yourself from crowds, often resulting in more fish being caught.

When on private land, treat it as if it were your own...maybe better. Remember, your actions can impact anglers for years, even generations, to come. With that in mind, some of my best bank-angling experiences have come from private lands.

It's a good idea to knock on doors early when looking for a place to fish, before the season starts or prior to actually getting on the water. This shows landowners you are serious about fishing, and it carries a good deal of respect, reflecting the fact that if you're willing to go to such effort prior to actually fishing that you'll likely respect the land once you start fishing on it.

Some of the better bank-fishing hotspots along any given stream can require a bit of a hike. To learn where these places are, talk to local resources. Sporting-goods store personnel, gas-station workers, restaurant employees, fish and wildlife, as well as fish-hatchery agents are all excellent resources. Ask where the best bank fishing is on your target waters and how to access it. People, especially fellow anglers, can be a great help in pointing you in the right direction.

Two options that can lead to increased bank-fishing opportunities are camping and rafting. Some of my best fishing experiences in Alaska have come where we hiked, camped, fished, and kept hiking the next day. This allows you to distance yourself from crowds, often resulting in more fish being caught and the tranquil

wilderness experience most of us earn for.

Hiking and pitching a tent is one way to gain access to more remote waters. Utilizing cabins is another. In Alaska, for instance, the U.S. Forest Service has several cabins in place along many streams. These cabins are open to the public, can be rented for a reasonable fee and allow you to access fantastic

Some of the better bank-fishing hotspots can require a bit of a hike.

fishing waters others will struggle to reach every day. Driving and staying in a camper or trailer is another option when it comes to overnighting on the river.

While there's no question drift boats open up a vast amount of water that bank anglers can't reach,

It took some river exploration to discover the pool that held this summer steelhead. Once found it produced numerous hookups.

it doesn't mean you have to own one of these boats to float a river. Pontoon boats and rafts can be used to gain access to more bank-fishing opportunities. You don't have to fish from these vessels; use them as a source of transportation to get you into places you otherwise would not be able to access.

Exploring a river from a boat allows you to see exactly what it's like. Discovering new holes to fish, marking them with reference points to land, then returning to them on foot, is just one of the benefits floating a river can lend. If you don't have a boat or raft, tubing a river in the warm days of summer can help you locate future fishing sites.

The Guided Option

Hire a guide for bank fishing? You bet. Though there are very few guides who actually hire-out on bank-fishing trips, they can teach you a lot. For the best bang for your buck, however, I suggest booking a trip or series of trips with a guide who will take you fishing from a boat.

The reason you book a trip with a guide is to learn, and there's no shortage of information to take in. From reading water to learning where fish hold and travel, from deciding which approach to use and what gear should be employed and why, these are the things good guides do every day. These are

92

the guys, and gals, who are in the trenches day in and day out. They catch fish for a living, and if they don't consistently produce, they're out of a job.

When setting up a guided trip of this nature, where you're looking to learn valued information, be honest about it with your guide. Tell them exactly what you're looking for and why. Many anglers who book guided trips do so to get away from the office. These folks may not really care about learning anything, they just want to relax and have a good time. If you want something more from a guide, be sure to communicate that at the onset.

I know of several anglers who book trips with guides on a regular basis, looking to learn something. You don't have to be a rookie to book a trip with a guide, either. I know of more than one seasoned

salmon and steelhead angler who books multiple trips each year with noted guides, just to learn the latest and greatest tricks.

General Hints

Generally speaking, a few other points bank anglers should consider are food and what to do with their catch. One of the reasons we fish is to catch fish to eat. Not only are salmon and steelhead tasty, they are some of the most nutrient-dense meat you can eat.

To attain the best-quality meat for eating purposes, the moment a fish is caught, snap the photos you need, bonk it on the head, then bleed the fish. This is easily done by snapping a gill rake, either with a knife, scissors or your finger. The purpose is to get as much blood as possible out of the fish, and since the blood has to pass through the

The reason you book a trip with a guide is to learn, and there's no shortage of information to take in.

One of the reasons we fish is to catch fish to eat. Not only are salmon and steelhead tasty, they are some of the most nutrient-dense meat you can eat.

gills, this is the most efficient way I know of.

Blood in fish coagulates fast, and this attracts bacteria that can taint the taste of fish, even once it's cooked. With the fish bled out, now it's important to get it cool. On hot days, if you've caught a fish and want to continue fishing, get it hanging in the coolest place possible. If there is no shade and you're not far from the rig, it may be worth taking a cooler of ice along, so you can get the fish cooling as quickly as possible. Avoid placing the fish in the river during warm times, as the water will actually cause the meat to spoil.

If spending all day on the river, and you've taken a lunch break, be sure and clean your hands before getting back to fishing. Grease from foods can be transferred not only to terminal gear, but to lines and other surfaces, all of which can keep a fish, especially salmon, from biting. Avoid eating greasy foods like fried chicken and potato chips while on the river, as these are some of the worst for transferring unwanted oils to your gear. Once done eating, wash your hands with soap or hand sanitizer to ensure all potentially foul odors are gone.

Conclusion

The art of bank fishing for salmon and steelhead is an enjoyable one to try and master. With the many ever-changing variables involved, it's actually a sport few have ever perfected, at least that I'm aware of. I know I'm a long ways from doing that, for the simple reason there's always something to learn.

What I've found in the world of fishing is once you think you've got it figured out, the fish are almost certain to prove otherwise. Sportfishing pits humans against nature, and there's no way of telling what nature or its animals will do 100% of the time. That's what makes this sport so enjoyable, so addicting.

Through hard work, dedication and a willingness to experiment with new ideas, anyone can learn how to become a successful bank angler. Keeping an open mind is crucial to finding success, it allows you to cover all the bases, rather than lose sight by focusing on only a few specific elements.

However you choose to learn the aspects of bank fishing, have a good time. Enjoy where you are at on the way to where you are going. I've been fishing salmon and steelhead for decades and have accepted the fact that I'll never learn all there is to know about these wonderful fish.

Enjoy your time on the water, and the resources we are so blessed to have. I've been fortunate to travel much of the world, and I can tell you, there aren't many places on this planet that have what we have in terms of public land access and outdoor opportunities.

I'm often asked, given the countries I've visited and the exotic places I've lived, why do I choose to live in Oregon. The answer is simple. This is where both my wife and I grew up and where we want to raise our two sons. Where else in the world can you fish for salmon and steelhead, year-round?

About The Author

Since the mid-1960s, Scott Haugen has been catching salmon and steelhead throughout the Pacific Northwest's breathtaking rivers. Today, Haugen makes his living as a television host, writer and lecturer. He normally spends more than 250 days a year in the field, and his greatest reward is sharing what he's learned.

A former science teacher of 12 years, Haugen has lived in and traveled to some of the world's most exciting places. Still, his passion for fishing, hunting and being in the outdoors, brings him back to where he grew up in western Oregon. It's where Scott, his wife, Tiffany, and their two sons, Braxton and Kazden, have chosen to make their home.

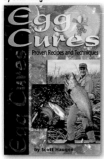